D1643422

- MAY 2003

GREATER CHINA
Political Economy, Inward Investment and Business Culture

GREATER CHINA

Political Economy, Inward Investment and Business Culture

edited by

CHRIS ROWLEY and MARK LEWIS

FRANK CASS • LONDON

First published in 1996 in Great Britain by
FRANK CASS AND COMPANY LIMITED
Newbury House, 900 Eastern Avenue, London IG2 7HH, England

and in the United States of America by
FRANK CASS
c/o ISBS, Inc.
5804 N.E. Hassalo Street, Portland, Oregon 97213-3644

British Library Cataloguing in Publication Data
A catalogue record for this book is available from the British Library.

ISBN 0 7146 4739 X (hbk)
ISBN 0 7146 4296 7 (pbk)

Library of Congress Cataloging-in-Publication Data

Greater China : political economy, inward investment, and business
culture / edited by Chris Rowley and Mark Lewis.
    p. cm.
    "First appeared in a special issue of [Asia Pacific business
review, vol. 2, no. 3 (Spring 1996)] "--T.p. verso.
    ISBN 0-7146-4739-X (hc). -- ISBN 0-7146-4296-7 (pbk.)
    1. China--Economic conditions--1976- 2. Economic forecasting-
-China. 3. Investments, Foreign--China. 4. Taiwan--Economic
conditions--1975- 5. Economic forecasting--Hong Kong.
I. Rowley, Chris, 1959-- . II. Lewis, Mark, 1965-
HC427.92.G73 1996
330.951--dc20
                             96-2924
                             CIP

This group of studies first appeared in a Special Issue of Asia Pacific
Business Review, Vol.2, No.3 (Spring 1996), [Greater China: Political
Economy, Inward Investment and Business Culture]

Printed in Great Britain by
Antony Rowe Ltd.

Contents

Abstracts

Greater China at the Crossroads? Convergence, Culture and Competitiveness *by Chris Rowley and Mark Lewis*

All those interested in international business and geo-politics are now conscious of globalization, regionalism and convergence. Despite the diplomatic tensions in the Asia Pacific region, links of trade and investment are seemingly drawing nations closer. Trade with mainland China has been central to economic growth in Hong Kong and Taiwan which, in turn, has led to the investment in China and its consequent economic development. However, economic factors, as well as political uncertainty, ultimately place limits on the development of closer regional integration. It is thus fair to ask whether business practices and objectives among the established and newly emerging enterprises of Greater China are as homogeneous or as predestined towards convergence as certain commentators contend. On the one hand, some recent studies argue for the validity of cross-national comparisons and similarities between ethnic Chinese, and emphasize that such similarities can only be reinforced by foreign direct investment and joint ventures within and between companies from the different regions of Greater China. On the other hand, however, the extent to which perceived similarities in economic practice and performance across Greater China are attributable to culture *per se* is questionable. In particular, the fashionable theoretical notion of 'economic culture' is open to question, as is, consequently, the belief in continued convergence between the regions of Greater China in accordance with a common 'Chinese economic culture'. Indeed, continued convergence will be constrained by institutional factors which seem likely to persist as central causes of difference in business practice and organization. Nowhere is this more apparent than in the case of industrial relations, with its wide-ranging influence on business–state relationships, competitive advantage, and economic-growth pathways.

The Political Economy of Greater China *by Tsang Shu-ki*

Since 1979, China has made tremendous progress in its economic reforms, and in these developments Hong Kong and Taiwan have beeen most deeply involved, so much so that the three economies have been collectively called 'Greater China'. This article investigates the integration process from the perspective of the political economy, pointing out the promises as well as the problems. The author is cautiously optimistic about the future, provided that far-sightedness can prevent any dominant urge for short-term profits and political compulsion. The logic of economic interests seems power enough to ensure that even the more formidable political barriers can eventually be overcome. As a result, Greater China looks likely to be increasingly open to the rest of the world.

Foreign Direct Investment in China: An examination of the literature by Stefan Kaiser, David A. Kirby and Ying Fan

Since 1978, when China announced its 'open-door' policy to pursue the country's long-term national goal, the *Four Modernisations*, more than 220,000 foreign funded ventures have been approved. By the end of 1994 some US$300 billion of contracted investment had been agreed and US$95 billion of utilized investment, making the country the most important recipient of foreign direct investment (FDI) in the developing world. This paper analyses the phenomenon of FDI in China. It examines the different forms and composition of FDI, reviewing its development since the early days of the 'open-door' policy and analysing its importance for Chinese domestic and export industries, as well as Western investor companies. Furthermore, the paper focuses on the world-wide sources of FDI in China and its distribution by both region and industry. Additionally, it reviews the existing research on FDI in China, emphasizing the investment mode of equity joint venture.

Inequality, Inflation and their Impact on China's Investment Environment in the 1990s and Beyond by Zhao Xiaobin Simon and Tong S.P. Christopher

Inequality, inflation, and unemployment have become increasingly explosive problems in today's China. In conjunction with an analysis of the spatial pattern of inflation, this paper examines the current trend of China's spatial disparities, in terms of economic output, real consumption, and real income, within inter-provincial, inter-regional and urban-rural framework. This paper also investigates the combined effect of the current high rate of inflation and spatial disparity on China's investment and business environment in the 1990s. Findings of this paper suggest that inter-regional inequalities in economic development and income distribution, especially since 1990, have been accelerated/exacerbated by high inflation, which appears to hit the poorer areas disproportionally. Given the reinforcement of disparity and inflation and the current upsurges of rampant localism, the investment and business environment of China in the 1990s, in terms of political and social unrest and economic profitability, will be severely undermined and will, therefore, become increasing uncertain. It is likely that this trend will extend beyond the millenium and last at least until the early 2000s.

Hermes Revisited: A Replication of Hofstede's Study in Hong Kong and the UK *by Sid Lowe*

Hofstedes' well-known study of cross-cultural values has come to be regarded as among the most influential in the field, and the subsequent extensive citation of a study, which involved the measurement of international differences in cultural values within IBM or 'Hermes', is testimony to its seminal status. Unfortunately, this success has not been matched by increased co-operative research amongst social scientists into cultural issues, namely through an 'intersubjective' approach which was one of Hofstede's hopes for subsequent development. Hofstede's approach, based on the comparative explanation of work-related values, is categorized and labelled variously and using different typologies, thus re-emphasizing that his approach is not the only perspective.

Culture's Consequences for Management in Hong Kong *by Sid Lowe*

In a recent review of Hofstede's comparative study of business practice and national cultures, 61 works replicating his methods are identified, and the critical four differences in the cultural dimension are ' largely confirmed'. The only replication of Hofstede's study within IBM (his original sample vehicle) has largely validated the original model some twenty years later. These results seem to confirm the valuable contribution of Hofstede's work, although his model contains the limitations of all models; the simplification of reality into an understandable form cannot do justice to its complexity. In this paper, the main consequences of Hofstede's work for Hong Kong are reviewed. His proposition that culture and particularly social values influence economic activity and management, which is consequently 'culture-bound', is restated and supported by more recent studies.

Greater China at the Crossroads?
Convergence, Culture and Competitiveness

CHRIS ROWLEY and MARK LEWIS

INTRODUCTION

The focus of this special issue – the possible (but problematic) emergence of so-called 'Greater China' encompassing mainland China, Taiwan, and Hong Kong – and the subject matter covered – economic reforms, inward investment, spatial disparities, and business culture – are topical and important. Not many days pass when these countries or issues do not appear in the news for a range of reasons, including the development of economic reforms, joint ventures, and trade.[1] What really 'catches the eye' concerns Greater China's economic growth rates and potential. The similarities, differences, underpinnings, results and prospects for the future of this are the main topics in this special issue.

All those interested in international business and geo-politics are now conscious of globalization, regionalism and convergence.[2] Despite the diplomatic tensions of the South China Sea, links of trade and investment are drawing the nations of the region together.[3] Hong Kong's political future is to be decided by the momentous event of 1997; the relationship between the People's Republic of China and the Republic of China, Taiwan is dominated by a mixture of practical accomodation and bellicose postures. The world has yet to see if vested interests emerge as the dominant force of Greater China, either within an enlarged mainland that will soon incorporate Hong Kong, or between the governments of Beijing and Taipei. Trade with China has been central to economic growth in Hong Kong and Taiwan, which, in turn, has led the investment in China and its consequent economic development.[4] Yet disparities within the mainland – the very unevenness of growth – are rarely highlighted.[5] Economic factors, as well as political uncertainty, place limits on development and regional integration. It is fair to ask, moreover, if business objectives amongst the established and new enterprises of Greater China are homogeneous or at least converging. Recent studies continue to demonstrate the validity of cross-national comparisons and similarities between ethnic Chinese, presumably reinforced by foreign direct investment (FDI) and joint ventures. It is equally certain that other, institutional, factors will persist as central causes of difference in business practice and organization. Nowhere is this more apparent than the case of industrial relations, with its wide-ranging

Chris Rowley and Mark Lewis, Royal Holloway, University of London influence on business–state relationships, competitive advantage, and economic growth pathways.)

It is with a view to providing a contextual introduction to these topics that the present article has been written. It is structured around a further six main parts. A brief summary of the main perspectives and points of the pieces that make up this volume is followed by a critical review of several of the different analytical perspectives from which it is possible to view developments in Greater China. Given its current high profile in the debates, especial attention is here paid to the theoretical validity of the cultural perspective. Culture has already been used to explain successful economic development in Japan and the 'East Asian Tigers', and for this reason its intuitive appeal as far as explaining competitiveness within, and convergence between, the regions of Greater China is obvious enough. Yet the fashionable notion of 'economic culture' on which all culturalist arguments are ultimately based is open to question and is here subjected to theoretical scrutiny. A section on the nature of international competition and aspects of industrial relations is then presented, followed by possible routes to economic development. Finally, some concluding points are made.

PERSPECTIVES

Tsang Shu-ki analyses reforms and integration in Greater China from the perspective of political economy The changes were based on a 'twin-track' approach whereby internal restructuring of the economy was combined with exposure to global trade winds and investment. The triangular linkages between mainland China, Taiwan and Hong Kong, and the places and levels of inward investment, are analysed. The phenomenal growth rates, rapid economic integration, and the problems, prospects and repertoire of possible outcomes are given, some of which we return to later. An optimistic scenario is presented in that the power of economic interests in an increasingly open Greater China can potentially overcome political barriers. However, the emergence of China's 'economic warlordism', with the development of interest groups which vie for concessions from central government but resist its command, is a demonstration of one particular difficulty.

Kaiser *et al* continue with the theme of inward investment in China at greater length. The different forms of FDI, composition (especially in joint ventures), sources (notably from Hong Kong and Taiwan), distribution and concentration in coastal areas, historical ebbs and flows, and the importance for domestic and export industries, are all examined.

Zhao and Tong then analyse the impact of inward investment and economic growth on China. They are particularly concerned with spatial disparities in output, consumption and income. Regional disparities have grown since the 1990s, reversing the generally equalizing trend of the 1980s and, although average real consumption per capita has increased, the inequality of distribution in China has also grown. The authors review attempted curbs on inflation via austerity policies, which have lead to 'stop–go' and recurrent inflation. Inflation in mainland China evidently has an 'administrative' nature, being rooted in deep-seated systemic failures. These developments have boosted the spread of 'active localism' and the weakening of central influence and control, causing political tension. The country is extraordinarily unequal, in terms of the urban–rural income differential ratio and by the standard of other developing Asian countries, and this inequality gap is still enlarging. Given the established relationships between high growth and declining inequality in Japan, the 'Four Tigers' and newly industrializing economies of Thailand, Malaysia and Indonesia, China's structural difficulties are an economic, social and political obstacle.[6] A gloomy and apocalyptic conclusion is reached: the 'mutual reinforcement' of disparity and inflation will induce an upsurge of rampant localism, which in turn will erode the investment and business environment in terms of both political and social unrest and economic profitability.

Lowe's contributions are based on Hofstede's model originally applied to a study of cross-cultural values within IBM. Lowe re-examines cultural differences, in order to test the stability of the earlier profiles, and national distinctions, examining, for example, whether the individualism index increases with a country's wealth. The consequences of such analyses for Hong Kong's managers are dealt with in his second piece, as are various models of organizational structures which have resonance in a 'Hofstedian' perspective. He concludes that differences between cultures remain relatively stable, thus supporting Hofstede's expectations, and that management is culture-bound. Lowe deems models of organization and structure to be culturally contingent, and thus calls into question the ethnocentricity and universality of management theories. Yet Lowe also emphasizes, correctly in our view, that we need to recognize the importance of situational or contextual dimensions in management, and not to regard culture as deterministic of success. He outlines the characteristics of Hong Kong organizations based on linkages which are 'relationship-centred' and founded on beliefs in tradition, moral debt, co-operative 'industrial recipes' and wider cultural reference groups. Such factors allow networks and the formation of flexible and temporary organizations to exploit specific contacts, with these organizations disbanding on completion of their objectives as new opportunities present themselves. These organizations are dominated by family-based hierarchies, traditional structures which integrate interests in trust-based systems of loyalty and mutually beneficial support.

Such a view of organizations and their cultural and infrastructural milieu is well established. Yet, it has strong echoes of the dynamic 'Marshallian' industrial districts[7] that existed historically in parts of the UK (as in textiles, pottery, and so on) and which remain in parts of the so-called 'Third Italy', Germany, Japan, and even the US.[8] In other words, business and industrial networks based on mutually supportive relationships of trust are not unique to the cultural milieu where it is currently so fashionable to locate them – namely the cultural milieu of Chinese Confucianism – but rather these

networks have existed and continue to exist in many other national and
cultural traditions. In turn, this surely indicates that the business networks
of Greater China – networks that to a large extent underlie the region's
competitiveness and that explain increasing economic convergence within
the region – are not necessarily the result of cultural exceptionalism. Rather,
the ingredients of competitive success are determined by institutional,
structural and organizational elements and, not least, by state actions. These
vary across, and even within, areas of Greater China.

ANALYTICAL APPROACHES

How might we approach an understanding of trade and business networks,
and management policy and practice, generally and specifically within
Greater China? How, that is to say, might we approach the study of the
underlying causes of competitiveness in the context of Greater China and
the prospects for economic convergence across the region? Various
approaches have been developed to account for similarities and differences
between countries in terms of economic practices and economic
performance. We will examine four main views. On the one hand, these
emphasize either structural characteristics (convergence and contingency
theory); on the other they give greater weight to cultural factors (ideational
and institutional approaches).[9] These will be dealt with in turn, although the
constraints of space (and the particular focus of two of the articles in this
volume) result in a circumscribed account of the former[10] compared with the
latter approach. The underlying premise of our analysis is that an approach
to Greater China based on the comparative method potentially offers the
most fruitful perspective from which to analyse economic developments in
the region, though the need for an awareness of the advantages and
drawbacks of this method, at different levels of analysis and through a
variety of questioning perspectives, is emphasized throughout.

Back to the Future: Towards Convergence?

First, there are ideas linked to convergence theory. Simply put, this assumes
that the process of industrialization and the use of advanced technology
move all countries towards similar systems.[11] An implication of this
approach is that there are 'universal truths' that can be applied. However,
whilst this view was very popular in the 1960s, it has received considerable
criticism. This is partly because it over-simplifies industrial development
and gives too much emphasis to the impact of technology.

A view within this broad approach, grouped around the label of
contingency theory, developed to meet some of these criticisms, and it
recognized that practices could be affected by factors such as differences in
technology or the stability of the organizational environment.[12] However,
these contingent factors still seemed to impose a rational logic of
administration and organization.

Such universalistic views of this nature continue to appear. For example, similar approaches are implicit in such famous and influential books as *In Search of Excellence*, *The Second Industrial Divide*, and more recently in *The Machine that Changed the World.*[13] Indeed, the hype surrounding similar ideas remains highly visible. Yet a major criticism of such theorists is that they fail to understand that the way managerial ideas and practices are interpreted and implemented varies between countries. Arguments which focus on such differences have given greater emphasis to cultural or institutional factors in accounting for divergence.

Durable Diversity: Cultural Characteristics and Institutions

A second broad approach, then, is a cultural one. The debate over the impact of culture on the economic competitiveness of nations and on economic convergence between nations contains many theoretical difficulties, not the least of which is the definition of culture itself. One problem with culture is that it can become a 'black box' which is used to explain all. Culture is generally taken to be the collective programming of the mind-set of members of a group which is then reflected in assumptions, beliefs and norms held in common by that group. It is because values and relations of the familial, societal and contractual kind are so important to human beings everywhere that many commentators have emphasized differences in culture as an explanatory variable of national economic performance. In particular, a large body of literature has emerged in recent years that attributes the phenomenal economic success of Japan and the 'East Asian Tigers' to a common cultural heritage that has brought about convergence between these countries in terms of their economic practices. Moreover, the culturalist perspective is now increasingly being used to analyse economic developments in the People's Republic of China itself. As a result, and since it appears, on the surface at least, to offer an intuitively persuasive explanation of the competitiveness of Greater China and of the prospects for intra-regional economic convergence, the culturalist approach is perhaps worth examining in more detail. In particular, the methodological procedure of culturalist approaches warrants critical examination.

For analysts of a culturalist persuasion, the success of Japan and later Hong Kong, Singapore, South Korea, Taiwan and, most recently, the People's Republic of China as well, is fundamentally, if not exclusively, to be explained in terms of certain well-entrenched cultural traits inspired by the Confucian tradition that is common to all these societies. Indeed, because certain core Confucian values appear intuitively linked to economic behaviour, they are seen by some commentators to form the basis of a common East Asian 'economic culture', different in certain essential features from that of the West.[14] According to this view, the East Asian development experience has been sufficiently different from that of the West to constitute a new model of capitalism, a 'second case' as Berger[15] has called it. The culturalist hypothesis allows for national variations within a common East Asian economic culture – Japanese economic culture, for example, will differ in some respects from that of South Korea – but considers the similarities more important than the differences. 'Neo-Confucianism' is thus held to explain the rise of these countries in much the same way as Weber saw the Protestant ethic as the key to understanding the much earlier industrialization and modernization of Western Europe.[16]

The cornerstone of culturalist explanations of economic behaviour is thus the concept of economic culture. Indeed, as one of the leading proponents of the Neo-Confucian paradigm of East Asian economic development makes clear, the notion of 'economic culture' is the starting point of all cultural explanations of economic performance: 'What, then, is the theoretical approach I want to propose here? It is expressed in a key concept recurring in various parts of the book – the concept of "economic culture".'[17] Given its critical importance in the culturalist hypothesis, then, it is important that we understand precisely what is meant by the term economic culture.

In broad terms, economic culture refers to the 'social, political, and cultural matrix or context within which particular economic processes operate',[18] but since many social, political and cultural factors are functionally neutral with regard to economic behaviour, and so have little or no impact on economic performance, it is clear that in a narrower sense the term economic culture must refer specifically to those socio-cultural values and attitudes that appear in some way to be intuitively linked to the economic process. Those socio-cultural values and attitudes that seem linked to economic behaviour are typically those that relate to education, thrift, deferred gratification and so forth, and it is because societies in the Confucian tradition are seen to exhibit common attitudes in such areas – attitudes that are different from those of the West – that a common East Asian economic culture is posited, an economic culture distinct from that of the West. For Berger, the distinctiveness of East Asian economic culture means that 'East Asia has generated a new type, or model, of industrial capitalism.'[19] It is for this reason that the validity of culturalist explanations of East Asian competitiveness on the one hand, and of convergence in economic practices between the different nations of the region on the other, ultimately rests on the theoretical integrity of this concept of economic culture.

The question, though, is how valid this notion of distinct economic cultures really is. If it can be shown a priori that different countries and peoples do indeed possess different economic cultures – values and attitudes that predispose them to behave in a distinct manner in the economic realm – then the culturalist hypothesis may well be as powerful an explanation of East Asia's economic success as it is possible to give. Equally, if a direct link can be empirically observed to exist between culture and economic performance after the event – if, in other words, it can convincingly be shown that different nations possess distinct economic cultures on an a posteriori basis – then, by the same token, culturalist hypotheses of economic performance will be strongly reinforced.

A methodological problem posed from the outset to a priori notions of economic culture is the fact that national cultures are *sui generis* – they are the result of specific circumstances unique to a given country or people, and as such can only be properly understood by means of systemic, as opposed to comparative, analysis.[20] Culture, like language, is a self-referential *system*, and this raises serious theoretical difficulties concerning the notion of economic culture as posited on an *a priori* basis as, for example, in the influential work of Hofstede.[21] Hofstede argues that differences in values between cultures require organizational responses, and that the nature of economic activity in a country will thus be determined to a large extent by the cultural values that prevail there. Hofstede wanted to quantify the influence of cultural factors on economic activity, and devised a schema to compare the cultural values of forty different countries. His procedure, however, is not to examine each individual culture in terms of its own systemic uniqueness, but rather to devise an *a priori* framework comprising four stylized socio-cultural variables that are then used as benchmarks against which to analyse each of the forty countries. The assumption underlying Hofstede's schema is that all cultures are equally susceptible to analysis in the same abstractly preconceived terms, and the four variables he uses as benchmarks are: 'power distance' (the extent to which members of a society accept a hierarchical or unequal power structure); 'uncertainty avoidance' (how members of a society cope with the uncertainties of everyday life); 'individualism' (the extent to which individuals perceive themselves as independent and autonomous beings, free from group pressure to conform); and 'masculinity' (the extent to which a society is inclined towards aggressive and materialistic behaviour).

So, the Japanese emphasis on uncertainty avoidance and social stability may require guarantees of job security, while Anglo-American economies are based on a high degree of labour market mobility that indicates peoples' willingness to accept greater uncertainty about future employment possibilities. Anglo-Saxon individualism encourages personal incentives, but Japanese collectivism remunerates group achievement and minimizes pay differentials. In concluding that organizations are 'culture-bound', Hofstede believes that there are no universal answers to the problems of organization and management, a finding Lowe in this volume concurs with. As is perhaps only to be expected, Hofstede ends up with forty distinct 'national economic cultures', because each of the forty countries studied responds differently along each axis and is thus located in a unique position within his overall four-dimensional schema.

Notwithstanding the interesting insights it delivers, Hofstede's schema is problematic because its premise is that certain values and attitudes can be abstractly preconceived in a vacuum and then tested for with equal validity in all cultural systems. In other words, *a priori* schemas such as Hofstede's sometimes run the risk of disregarding the unique systemic integrity of distinct national cultures and, as a result, of making the unjustified implication that like values in one culture are being compared with like values in another culture.[22]

Unlike Hofstede, who begins with preconceived socio-cultural values as his variables, those who argue for a link between culture and economic performance on an *a posteriori* basis take as their starting point the historical economic performance of a given nation or nations. They observe that this nation (or nations) is based on a certain cultural tradition, and it is then contended that certain values and attitudes within this tradition are intuitively linked to economic performance. As a result, a national economic culture is posited *a posteriori* as a hypothesis that might explain the economic success or failure of the nation in question. The empiricism inherent in this methodology makes *a posteriori* notions of economic culture more readily appealing than the *a priori* conception offered by Hofstede. After all, by examining real, as opposed to preconceived, values and attitudes, they would seem to respect the systemic integrity of national cultures. Nonetheless, *a posteriori* notions of economic culture pose their own theoretical problems, the most salient of which is that because they are offered after the event they must, by definition, locate cultural values in some kind of historical perspective. So, at issue is the extent to which cultural adaptation is allowed for in the face of social, political and economic change.

Two broad responses to this problem of historical perspective can be discerned in the culturalist literature. On the one hand, there exists the radical *a posteriori* position, whereby national culture is considered to be a more or less intrinsic and unchanging feature of a country or people. Certain culturalist accounts of Japanese economic success appear to adopt this kind of radical approach. Since it was the first non-Western nation to industrialize, attempts to locate the country's economic success in traditional values and attitudes unique to Japan[23] are to be expected, the premise of such studies being that traditional Japanese values were unaffected by modernization:

> The rapid transformations of the traditional feudal system into a modernized nation proceeded without involving the process of 'individualization' of the people through breaking out of the cohesive traditional culture. By the functions of 'natural' and 'ideological transferability', Japan was modernized without destroying basic archetype cultural values.[24]

From this premise it is then argued that Japan's traditional values proved particularly conducive to rapid and successful industrialization, a recurrent theme being the need for group cohesion and collective identity. On this reading, Japan's traditional cultural traits were, following the Meiji restoration in 1868, transferred to its emerging industries, and it is thus to 'the pre-industrial values of Japan', as the subtitle of Bellah's[25] famous work has it, that we must turn if we are to understand the country's economic modernization and its spectacular performance since 1945.

There is, however, an obvious problem with this first, Japan-specific, culturalist argument: it too easily equates the beliefs and values of the

Tokugawa shogunate with modern-day Japan. It is based on the radical culturalist assumption that cultural values and attitudes are intrinsic and unchanging, and it thus tends tautologically to posit a causal link between cultural values and economic performance *post hoc*, while leaving many other factors that may in fact be more directly relevant to economic performance unexplored. For example, Ketcham[26] associates the management systems of Japanese companies with the high degree of commitment demonstrated by their employees. This commitment in the workplace is deemed to be a defining feature of Japanese companies, an integral part of their success, derived from an 'embedded' Confucian tradition of loyalty and mutual obligation. On this reading, it is then hard to accept the transferability of these systems to other countries,[27] with the result that Japan's economic success is held to have its roots in a distinctly Japanese economic culture. However, this quality of 'commitment' is all too often blithely *assumed* to be a culturally-determined feature of the Japanese workplace, while other possible explanations go unexplored. Consequently, the conclusion that suggests itself is that the culturalist argument in this case rests on a *post hoc propter hoc* reasoning process.[28]

On the other hand, there exists a more pragmatic *a posteriori* culturalist viewpoint, which consciously attempts to avoid the charge of naive *post hoc* reasoning. This approach rests on the notion that Japanese and East Asian economic success is based on a common Neo-Confucian economic culture. Following the economic success of other East Asian nations – Hong Kong, South Korea, Singapore and Taiwan – many writers have drawn attention to the fact that they share common features inspired by Confucianism: the work ethic, frugality, reverence for learning and collectivism inspired by Confucianism.[29]

These studies are perhaps more sophisticated than culturalist arguments based on pre-industrial traditions because they more readily accommodate the fact that culture adapts as a response to economic, political and social considerations: they recognize, in other words, that national cultures can undergo change. For one thing, proponents of the Neo-Confucianist paradigm are more explicit in their recognition of the debt owed to the West by Japan and other East Asian countries, and it is recognized that without the technical expertise imported from the much more technologically advanced West, Japan and later other East Asian countries, would never have been able to achieve the industrial transformation that made their phenomenal post-war growth record possible in the first place.[30] Yet, whilst it is admitted that the technological preconditions of economic growth first came from abroad, it is argued that socio-cultural values peculiar to Confucianism have combined with this foreign technology to produce a differentiated and arguably more powerful model of capitalist development than that of the West. Khan,[31] for example, states that 'societies based upon the Confucian ethnic ways may be superior to the West in the pursuit of industrialization, affluence and modernization', and that Confucian ways 'will result in all the neo-Confucian societies having higher growth rates than other cultures'.

For proponents of the Neo-Confucian paradigm, then, cultural factors have been instrumental in the phenomenally successful post-war economic growth and development records of certain East Asian countries and peoples (Japan, Hong Kong, Singapore, South Korea, Taiwan, The People's Republic and the overseas Chinese communities present in many South East Asian countries). Weber's Protestant ethic here finds an echo in Confucian traditions that are, it is argued, equally conducive to capital formation and economic modernization. The most prominent features of Confucianism in this respect are: the value placed on thrift and asceticism; respect for learning and education; familial bonds that emphasize respect for one's elders and responsibility to one's juniors; and a belief in the nobility of self-sacrifice in the interests of the larger number's wellbeing. The culturalist interpretation of East Asian development[32] thus holds that thrift and asceticism account for high successive annual rates of investment in the post-war era, whilst reverence for learning explains highly trained and highly skilled workforces. Harmonious employee relations are held to mirror Confucian family ties in so far as labour respects management and management looks after labour, and people's willingness to subordinate individual gain to the good of the nation allows national economic policy to be oriented to the long term.

The problem with this view, though, is that economic culture in this case becomes a 'catch-all' device, one that is general and flexible enough to accept that culture undergoes change but to maintain nonetheless that it is instrumental in determining economic performance. In other words, this position sometimes verges on wanting the argument both ways and may, as a result, itself be little more than a convenient, albeit more sophisticated, *ex post* rationalization. Consider, for example, the position of Berger.[33] On the one hand, he accepts that economic change causes cultural change, giving as an example the trend away from collective values in Japan and East Asia in the aftermath of industialization:

> (...) the cross-national evidence on individuating modernity is strong enough to make one very sceptical about the ability of these societies to continue on their merry course of happy 'groupism'. The values of individual autonomy are undermining East Asian communalism and are likely to continue doing so.

On the other hand, he insists on the importance of culture in explaining East Asia's success in the industrialization process and, moreover, argues that East Asia's success would not have been so telling if other cultural norms had held sway in the region:

> Specific elements of East Asian civilization, be it in the 'great tradition' or in folk culture, have fostered these values and have consequently given the societies of the region a comparative advantage in the modernization process. (...) it is inherently implausible to believe that Singapore would be what it is today if it

were populated, not by ethnic Chinese, but by Brazilians or Bengalis
– or, for that matter, by a majority of ethnic Malays.[34]

When juxtaposed in this manner, such extracts demonstrate Berger's
position to be an uncertain compromise, an attempt to avoid the charge of
naivety in arguing the case for East Asia's cultural exceptionalism whilst at
the same time making a claim for the influence of culture on the region's
stunning post-war economic performance. As he does not seriously explore
any of the many other possible reasons for East Asia's successful
modernization, however, it is a compromise that is ultimately based on the
same *post hoc* reasoning process as that of those commentators who adopt
a more radical culturalist position.

As they are offered after the event, then, *a posteriori* culturalist
explanations of economic performance, whether radical or pragmatic, are
always potentially liable to the charge of *post hoc propter hoc* reasoning.
Unless they give due consideration to issues other than culture in their
investigations and so arrive at their conclusion by means of hard evidence,
we must be wary of the blithe assumptions to be found in some of the more
radical approaches, and the uncertain compromises to be found in some of
the more pragmatic approaches.

To summarize the argument presented in this section: national cultures
are uniquely configured systemic structures and this makes the isolation and
comparison of specific cultural attributes a hazardous enterprise. However,
the *a priori* notion of economic culture by definition overlooks this sytemic
nature of culture, for it assumes that individual cultural attributes –
specifically, those that are held to influence economic behaviour – *can* be
isolated and compared. By contrast, *a posteriori* notions of economic
culture, while generally mindful of the systemic nature of national cultures,
seem prone by their very nature to the temptation of *post hoc* reasoning.
In short, culturalist arguments would appear to overstate the case. For
instance, can all differences be explained in terms of people's attitudes? East
Asian companies have established successful operations throughout many
parts of the world using indigenous workers who have a wide variety of very
different values. Too much emphasis may be given to history and individuals'
perceptions and it gives little account to how values change over time. For
example, if Western individualist ideas gain popularity in East Asia, what
effect will this trend have on traditional practices? Values on their own are not
enough. They need to be rooted in society's social and economic structure.
Some argue that culture includes not only the values held by individuals, but
also the relations between people at work and in families, as well as the
structure the firm and society.[35] Approaches which have tried to take account
of these broader factors are often referred to as institutional views.

This institutional approach argues for an understanding of the social and
economic institutions which support the continuation of traditional values
and practices.[36] For example, economic success may not be attributable
simply to factors such as a 'strong work ethic' and 'discipline', but to

comprehensive educational and vocational training creating a highly skilled workforce, complemented by consultative industrial relations systems and long term financial support from banking institutions and the local state (as in Germany) or state guidance, company unions and consultative practices (as in Japan). Basically, we cannot examine separate systemic aspects without location in the specific societal context. However, this sort of approach has been criticized for presenting a static view of national industrial order and for failing to recognize that a divergent and contradictory range of practices may exist within a society. There is no account of how change comes about, and little attention is paid to the role of the state.

The above analysis shows that a variety of perspectives exist. We need to remember which particular 'angle' authors may (often implicitly) be taking.

APPROACHES TO GREATER CHINA

Several initial contextual points need to be made, concerning comparative analysis (an undoubted need, but with problems); aggregation (as large differences, obviously, remain within Greater China); causality, and analytical level (enterprise, region, country, and so on); and location (indigenous firms, inward investors, joint ventures, multinational enterprises). These make for difficulties of labyrinthine complexity and opaqueness, not neat conclusions and clarity.

Some interesting comparative analysis using similar frameworks to those outlined earlier have been applied specifically to the areas within what we call Greater China (and other nations in the region). These include the following. Three schools of explanation in the field of human resource management (HRM) and the international transfer of systems from Japan to China have been outlined: culturalist; traditionalist; technology-HRM fit (a contingency perspective).[37]

A 'neo-institutionalist theory' has been used for understanding the nature of HRM.[38] This argues that the behaviour, technology and structure in organizations come into being, become accepted and are then widely used in different organizational and national settings. Such a perspective helps to identify developments in organizations and in nations, and to compare, contrast and integrate the patterns of practice across them.

Other work has outlined four approaches (to explaining the characteristics and trends in trade union movements).[39] These are: modernization theory (societies progress along a path of development in which economic forces play the major formative role in shaping social institutions); international labour market theory (with global capitalism companies dominating markets are transnational in scope and take advantage of low cost areas of production and transportation systems); a political science approach (the basic structure and purpose of trade unions are largely dependent on party systems); and political sociology perspective (the state is a central explanatory variable).

Three explanations of economic success in East Asia have been outlined in some recent work.[40] These are: the new culturalist; institutionalist; and an approach which stresses the role of 'actors' in the system. Such an account is not deterministic or suggestive of 'iron laws', but views outcomes of choices to be made in the light of either world economic developments or local cultural affinities. There is no sense of determinism and choices will be the outcome of indeterminate and complex political processes.

In short, a range of different perspectives have emerged and some have been used directly in relation to Greater China. These range from a convergence type view that over time Greater China will develop similarities to other industrialized states, through culturalist approaches, noting the 'peculiarity' of Greater China's history, beliefs, and so on, to institutionalist views, that structures and so on in Greater China will produce the area's own forms of organization. However, whichever view is taken, there can be a problem – that of partiality – some aspects seem to be underplayed, not least, that of industrial relations.

'THE MISSING FACES'?

At one time, theorists on the location of industry found explanation in the comparison of transport costs, production being optimally placed between sources of materials and markets.[41] There are similar ideas in the concept of an 'industrial life cycle' with migration around the world as production 'matures' in different countries.[42] Now, according to writers like Robert Reich,[43] capital moves freely across borders, transport costs are comparatively small compared to other factors, and production seeks either skilled or cheap labour.

Another 'missing face' is that of industrial relations and especially labour – and its interaction with other 'actors' (the state and employers) in the respective systems. This is a key aspect because industrial relations have a critical, but all too often underplayed or even forgotten, impact on routes to competition. Paradoxically, part of the problem is the current vogue for HRM as a subject, in which all too often industrial relations is removed (or at best de-emphasized) from the analysis. This weakness can be reduced by examining some contemporary comparative work (although we need to remember that HRM cannot be simply take as a surrogate for industrial relations) in this increasingly popular area.[44]

For example, several authors argue a fashionable line that a primary source of competitive advantage in the Pacifc Rim is the use of human resources. Some authors writing with regard to HRM in this area assert that the relationship between external and internal labour markets (whose interface is critically influenced by the state and organized labour) is associated with features of a firm's HRM system, the degree of bureaucratization and professionalization of HRM.[45] They argue that the least bureaucratic corporate HRM systems are in China (although the state does allocate labour), Hong Kong and Taiwan, while in terms of

professionalization, China is low, although Hong Kong is increasing in this
dimension.[46] However, we would concur with Warner's perceptive
conclusion that '...HRM is too culturally infused with Western values to be
as yet on the Chinese menu.'[47] Furthermore, the management of
employment in China's state-owned enterprises (SOEs) and the origins,
development and contemporary corrosion of the iron rice bowl approach,
as well as the 'three systems' reforms in personnel, wage systems, social
insurance, during the early 1990s, have been recently researched and
excellently analysed.[48] This work similarly concludes that we can question
whether Western style HRM has yet evolved in China; and, while it is
possible that Western type employment practices may be grafted on to the
current characteristics, producing a 'hybrid' form, there remains a gap
between intent and practice with organizational inertia.

Industrial relations does not exist in a vacuum, but interacts with wider
political, economic and social structures and culture. What are these like in
Greater China? The roots of Chinese management and its industrial
relations system can be seen in Kaple.[49] An excellent contemporary account
of the evolution, working and reform of management, employment and
organizations (and their decision making) is provided by Child in his
empirical work and research.[50] The mix of organizations in China include
SOEs open to various degrees of 'marketization', and joint ventures. It has
recently been reported that with worse than expected debts and losses in its
industrial sector, China has announced an intensification of its drive to
reform its SOEs, for example, there has been the unusual step of an
announcement of the dismissal, for bad management, of seven heads of
SOEs in the North Eastern industrial city of Shenyang.[51] Interestingly, to
help keep social peace, especially as labour surplus continues to increase
(exacerbated by further shifts from the countryside to conurbations and
rising consumer expectations), limits to reforms will be imposed: the labour
force in SOEs cannot be radically reduced for political reasons, therefore
their subsidies cannot be cut to help in inflation, so maintaining the costs of
the SOE's social infrastructures and limiting further reforms.[52]

What is the situation in the rest of what is seen as Greater China? In
Taiwan economic development has been underpinned by a variety of
factors.[53] Early on there was the creation of a state-controlled and enterprise-
based trade union organization, with welfare responsibilities being forced
on to employers. However, economic problems have emerged, including a
tight labour market, rising wages, and pressure to act more 'responsibly' in
trade relations. Taiwan's large trade surpluses and foreign reserves are now
being drawn upon in a state-led infrastructural development programme to
maintain growth and development. The importance of small and medium
size enterprises (SMEs), along with 'economic familism' and sub-
contracting (but with an absence of large firms and vertical integration) are
noted, as these enable production through 'satellite assembly systems'.
These dissolve when orders stop, then individual firms seek new orders and
reform systems. Therefore, they remain very sensitive to world market

conditions, demand and forces. In this way success is attributed to the dynamism and highly flexible small Chinese family owned sector (with similar arguments used for Hong Kong).

Likewise, Hong Kong is underpinned by a variety of factors.[54] Here the state has a minimalist role in guiding the economy, direction laying with the SMEs. Nevertheless, the government still had some role: limited, as in orchestrating the activities of business; but more significant, as on the supply side, particularly in the areas of infrastructure, education, social welfare and control of the supply of labour via immigration controls. However, the state has avoided attempts at directing the economy through SOEs in strategic areas or giving protection or preferential treatment. It combines the features of Chinese family business of paternalism (based on the hierarchical principles of Confucian social order) – family centredness but employer–employee distrust and extensive 'guanxi' networking, together with limited state intervention. As is argued: 'The Taiwanese state supports its Chinese family businesses in an attempt to overcome their weaknesses, the Hong Kong state does not.'[55]

The analysis in this section highlights the similarities, but also the substantial differences, in the political, economic and social structures and culture within Greater China. These, along with industrial relations, remain diverse. These provide imposing constraints on convergence or the impacts of globalization.

POSSIBLE ROUTES TO SUCCESS

The above analysis is important not simply to enhance our understanding, but also because it has key implications for routes to competition (and even public policy). Broadly, we can identify two rough models of competition: production based on technology-led, high value-added and sophisticated products, utilising expensive, but highly skilled and productive, workers; versus labour intensive, low value and simple products, using cheap, low skilled workers.[56] The role of labour and trade unions (and the state) in these routes is critical. For example, in some circumstances, powerful constraints restrict employers (as in Germany or Sweden) from competing by lowering employment costs. Labour is relatively costly and difficult to remove, but is well trained and productive. Therefore, employers tend to compete within those constraints and opportunities. Such a constellation of factors encourages companies to upgrade technology, invest in the latest techniques and use skilled labour in high value added work to compete – there is little choice. However, if labour is low cost, easy to 'hire and fire', and poorly trained, is it any wonder that firms do not make long-term investment in expensive capital equipment and employee development when they can quickly, easily and cheaply shed labour or reduce costs to boost short-term productivity and competitiveness? Yet this is an 'escalator' that once employers jump (or fall) on to is both difficult to get off and takes them to an unpleasant destination via a self-reinforcing, downward spiral of 'social dumping' and bidding down of labour protection.[57]

We can locate Greater China's labour and trade unions within such perspectives.[58] Its trade union systems have been categorized as: 'state corporatist' (China); and 'state exclusionary', with variants of 'autonomous, market' (Hong Kong) and 'transitional' (Taiwan). Chinese unionism reflects Communist Party ideology, which views unions as 'transmission belts' for the achievement of largely productionist goals. Furthermore, given the collapse of unionism in many of the former Communist regimes, even greater political reform does not necessarily bode well for unions. In Hong Kong, trade unions are subject to limited state control with state strategies aimed at maintaining close ties with business elites, although they are recognized by senior government officials as performing a useful function in the labour market as long as they are not a challenge to the *status quo*. Unions have low density and fragmented structures and are particularly weak in the private sector, which may reflect the impact of patriarchal and paternalistic forms of management and the efficacy of personal and community networks in resolving work-related problems. While there has been some development, such as the opportunity for trade union representatives to participate in the governance of Hong Kong in a quasi-corporatist political framework, this is very limited. Commonly presented post-1997 scenarios do not promise any enhanced independent role for trade unions. Trade unionism in Taiwan bears the imprint of both a repressive past and a more liberal present associated with the emergence of more democratic politics, although a problematic position is indicated as the trade union movement is dominated by the Chinese Federation of Labour, which is in effect an instrument of the government.

Given the above, it is unlikely that industrial relations, and in particular, trade unionism, in Greater China will play a significant role in terms of constructing blocks to routes to competition based on lowering employment and standards, so forcing companies to compete by upgrading technology and moving into higher value added production. Yet, it has already been noted that effective use of even today's high technology equipment (which itself is often only imported or copied from abroad) is a serious problem for China's organizations.[59] Similarly, Taiwan's SMEs face problems, including: their suboptimal scale and higher average costs; limited upgrading of production with technical innovation and movement into the highest value research and development intensive sectors; restricted investment in the most advanced capital equipment; and dependence on Japanese technology.[60] Indeed, in the next piece in this volume Tsang Shu-ki notes the worrying 'hollowing out' of Taiwanese industries as they shift from high technology routes and invest in 'sweatshop factories' in China. Likewise, Hong Kong is failing to advance technologically and to upgrade its manufacturing to higher value added activities, exacerbated by a decline in manufacturing and problems with both their employee relations and economic limitations (they only have short term relations with large firms and so face little demand to up-grade production facilities).[61] Its labour market is suffering from exceptionally high degrees of flexibility, weak organized labour, large numbers of immigrant workers, and abandonment by numerous professionals and the highly qualified. Also, as Tsang Shu-ki indicates, labour mobility has led to 'sectoral shifting' (from manufacturing to services) in Hong Kong. Critically, this 'flexibility' releases pressure for, as he puts it, 'climbing the technological ladder' and is a chimera as long term competitive capabilities are eroded.[62]

This is a worrying situation and scenario. Indeed, Krugman the famous US economist, evocatively and succinctly suggested in 1994 that the 'Asian Miracle' was based on 'perspiration rather than inspiration'.[63] We only need to look at the situation nearby to see what may well happen. Singapore is loosing low-skilled manufacturing to Malaysia and Indonesia. As even companies in Thailand are discovering, they cannot compete with China (or India) on labour costs alone when their wage levels are one quarter (and one fifth) of what Thai workers demand.[64] Such countries must 'trade up' to remain competitive, using more sophisticated manufacturing techniques, with all the concomitant aspects of state direction to boost the quality of labour, training, long term investment, and so on.

As the UK is discovering, the low labour cost route to competition is problematic and self-reinforcing, especially over the long term. It leads to competitive bidding down of labour costs and conditions in a 'virtueless circle'. As Winston Churchill implied when establishing the Wages Councils in Britain (to provide a 'safety net' in the so-called 'sweated trades') in the early part of the 20th Century – if such actions result in the loss of certain industries to lower labour cost areas, then so be it. Surely it is the 'inspiration' route that must be travelled over the long run? This stark choice may well need to be faced in Greater China sooner rather than later. However, it may be argued that this situation is being confronted in Taiwan (and Singapore), but less so in Hong Kong and that arguably mainland China may need to go through its low-cost development stage first.

CONCLUSION

How can we understand the various economic, political and social forces which currently influence development in the South China Seas? Of importance to this and aspects of the approaches revolving around culture and institutions. In particular, the role of the industrial relations system in terms of efficiency and productivity, and in this, the role of trade unions, employers and the state is critical. This has a partial echo of Dore's work of over 20 years ago, when the role of the state was stressed in his account of factory organization in Britain and Japan which emphasized their national–institutional distinctiveness.[65]

On the one hand, one could make a tentative case that convergence (under a new guise of globalization?) is occuring to some extent in Greater China. For example, on the one side mainland China is moving its moribund organizations from sclerotic state socialism towards operation within an increasingly market-driven reform economy, while from the other direction Taiwan, and to a lesser extent Hong Kong, may tone down the harshness of the winds of the free market and guide developments, such as to upgrade production. Will these meet in the 'middle'? As systems evolve, the history and context of industrial relations will become an increasingly important variable.

However, it would seem that ideas of convergence and universalism, for example, even in its modern variants, are overplayed. This is not to deny that there can be sharing and borrowing of ideas and practices, but that, as Elger and Smith perceptively point out, 'societal specificity' continues to be reproduced and preserved by agencies such as societal arrangements and institutions.[66] Indeed, for these authors, national uniqueness is '...created by socio-economic settlements between social agencies and institutions operating on a national terrain.'[67] In particular, they note institutional arrangements between capital and labour, state–firm relations, capital–capital relations and distinctive factory regimes within particular socieities, and which are '...less the consequence of cultural legacies than of socio-political action.'[68] Such perspectives provide a much needed and refreshing tonic to the over simplistic views of apostles of convergence and universalism.

Finally, a quite gloomy scenario may be presented of Greater China. It may well inceasingly compete by 'regression' on the 'downward escalator' with concomitant competitive bidding down of employment conditions. In particular, it is difficult to see China breaking out of this spiral, while Taiwan is having problems in its technological upgrading and a constrained labour movement, and Hong Kong is hitting economic turbulence as its labour market haemorrhages, with failure to upgrade technologically and move into higher value activities and weak trade unions. As the 'Pacific Age' emerges, labour organizations in the constituent areas of Greater China will remain constrained, and in their various ways they will act as 'transmission belts', rather than protecting labour, and in so doing will not be able to force employers to surmount the difficulties and barriers of competing in a different fashion. This is a rubicon that waits to be crossed.

ACKNOWLEDGMENTS

Many thanks to Robert Fitzgerald for his guidance and perceptive points on an earlier version of this article. The normal disclaimers apply.

NOTES

1. See, *inter alia*, J. Child, 'Exercising Strong Direction', *Financial Times* 6 November (1995), p.14; W. Dawkins, 'Principles of a Profitable Alliance', *Financial Times* 6 November (1995), p.14; M. Wolf, 'China's Socialist Market Economy', *Financial Times*, 13 November (1995), p.26; M. Wolf, 'The Iron Rice Bowl', *Financial Times China Survey*, 20 November (1995), p.IV; M. Wolf, 'A Country Divided by Growth', *Financial Times*, 20 February (1996), p.14; P. Montagnon, 'Focus Shifts to High-Tech Sectors', *Financial Times China Survey*, 20

November (1995), p.IV; G. Crothall, 'China Shakes Up State Companies', *Financial Times*, 19 December (1995), p.12.

2. However, ideas of convergence are contested, as noted later, while the concept of globalization can also be questioned. See, *inter alia*, P. Hirst and G. Thompson, *Globalization in Question* (Blackwell:1996).

3. Our thanks to Robert Fitzgerald for these points.

4. See P. Nolan, *China's Rise, Russia's Fall* (Macmillan:1996) for a comparison between evolutionary reform in China and catastrophic 'big bang' change in Russia (under the influence of economists and advisors in expensive clothes with high incomes and lap-top computers who made generalizations about 'correct' policy prescriptions to transform formely socialist economies).

5. However, Wolf (op. cit., 1996) shows that for some such inequality is not new or becoming worse. For example, see J. Tianlun, J. Sachs and A. Warner, 'Trends in Regional Inequality in China', *National Bureau of Economic Research Working Paper*, 5412 January (1996).

6. Thanks to Robert Fitzgerald for this point.

7. A. Marshall, *Principles of Economics* (Macmillan:1890, 8th ed.1986); A. Marshall, *Industry and Trade* (Macmillan:1919, 3rd ed. 1927). Also, see J. Chapman, *The Lancashire Cotton Industry* (Manchester University Press:1904).

8. See, *inter alia*, M. Piore and C. Sabel, *The Second Industrial Divide* (Basic Books:1984); C. Sabel, 'Flexible Specialization and The Re-Emergence of Regional Economies' in P. Hirst and J. Zeitlin (eds), *Reversing Industrial Decline?* (Berg:1989), pp.18–70; C. Sabel, G. Herrigel, R. Deeg and R. Kazis, 'Regional Prosperities Compared: Massachusetts and Baden-Wurttemberg in the 1980s', *Economy and Society*, Vol.18, No.4 (1989), pp.374–404; E. Goodman and J. Banford (eds), *Small Firms and Industrial Districts in Italy* (Routledge:1989); F. Pyke, G. Becattini, and W. Sengenberger (eds), *Industrial Districts and Inter-Firm Co-operation in Italy* (ILO:1990); M. Storper, 'Flexible Specialization and Regional Agglomeration: The Case of the US Motion Picture Industry', *Annals of the Association of American Geographers*, Vol.77, No.1 (1987), pp.104–17; M. Porter, *The Competitive Advantage of Nations* (Macmillan:1990).

9. See, *inter alia*, C. Lane, *Labour and Management in Europe* (Edwin Elgar:1989); I. Beardwell and L. Holden (eds), *HRM: A Comparative Perspective* (Pitman:1994).

10. However, see M. Lewis, R. Fitzgerald and C. Harvey, *The Growth of Nations* (Bristol Academic Press:1996); Hirst and Thompson, op. cit. for fuller accounts.

11. See F. Harbison and C. Myers, *Management in the Industrialised World* (McGraw-Hill:1959); C. Kerr, J. Dunlop, F. Harbison, and C. Myers, *Industrialism and Industrial Man* (Heinemann:1962).

12. See D. Pugh *et al.*, *Writers on Organizations* (Penguin: 1983); D. Pugh, *Organizational Theory* (Penguin:1984) for details.

13. T. Peters and R. Waterman, *In Search of Excellence* (Harper and Row:1982); Piore and Sabel, op. cit.; J. Womack, D. Roos, and D. Jones, *The Machine that Changed the World* (Rawson Associates:1990).

14. P. Berger, *The Capitalist Revolution: Fifty Propositions about Prosperity, Equality and Liberty* (Gower:1987); P. Berger and M. H. H. Hsiao (eds), *In Search of an East Asian Development Model* (Transaction Books:1986); H. Khan, *World Economic Development* (Westview Press:1979); Tai, Hung-Chao (ed), *Confucianism and Economic Development: An Oriental Alternative* (Washington Institute Press:1989); S. G. Redding, *The Spirit of Chinese Capitalism* (de Gruyter:1995). For studies relating specifically to China itself see E. F. Hartfield, 'The Divergent Economic Development of China and Japan', in Tai (ed), op. cit. pp.92–114; Y. Wong, 'Republic of China's Experiences with Economic Development', Ibid., pp.115–27.

15. Berger, op. cit. p.141.

16. M. Weber, *The Protestant Ethic and the Spirit of Capitalism* (Allen & Unwin:1930); M. Weber, *The Religion of China: Confucianism and Taoism* (Free Press:1951).

17. Berger, op. cit. p.7.

18. Ibid.

19. Ibid. p.144.

20. To illustrate this point, a useful analogy can be made with language. The words that make up the vocabulary of a given language are often assumed to be isolated entities that possess an intrinsic meaning, that intrinsic meaning being the object or phenomenon in the real world that is referred to by the word in question. In this view, each word in a language has equivalents in other languages that denote the same object or phenomenon in the real world

(for example English 'river' and French 'rivire' both denote a body of running water), and this makes translation between languages possible. However, the equivalence that is held to exist between words in different languages in this way is much weaker than might initially be imagined. To take the example of English 'river' and French 'rivire' again, although they both apparently denote the same phenomenon in the real world, they have different functions within their respective semantic systems. English 'river' is distinguished from words like 'stream' and 'rivulet' by virtue of the size of the body of water, whereas French 'rivire' is distinguished from other French words denoting flowing water like 'fleuve' by additonal considerations such as whether the body of water in question runs into the sea. In simple terms, the words 'river' and 'rivire' have different connotations, and are thus not exact equivalents. In short, the meaning of a word, as opposed to its denotation, can only be understood with reference to other words in the same semantic system. In precisely the same way, national cultures are best understood as complicated contextual structures, in which distinct values and attitudes do not exist in isolation, but rather in a well-defined relationship with other values and attitudes. [The analogy with language given here draws on J. Culler, *Saussure* (Fontana:1985), pp.23–34].

21. G. Hofstede, *Culture's Consequences* (Sage:1980).

22. Another author who attempted to posit an *a priori* schema for comparing different cultures was Weber's prominent disciple Talcott Parsons [T. Parsons, *The Social System* (The Free Press:1951), p.177]. He devised a framework of 'pattern variables' consisting of five diametrically opposed categories: 'affectivity vs. affective neutrality'; 'self-orientation vs. collectivity orientation'; 'universalism vs. particularism'; 'achievement vs. ascription'; and 'specificty vs. diffuseness'. Predictably enough, he then contended that the industrial occupational structure of the West is characterized by a 'system of universalistic-specific affectively neutral achievement-oriented roles', whereas Confucian values are diametrically opposed to 'the development of anything like capitalism'. The similarities in procedure between Parsons and Hofstede are evident, and it is interesting to note that Parsons' schema has been attacked by Glazer [N. Glazer, 'Social and Cultural Factors in Japanese Economic Growth', in H. Patrick and H. Rosovsky (eds), *Asia's New Giant: How the Japanese Economy Works* (The Brookings Institution:1976), pp.816–21] for similar reasons to those outlined in our critique of Hofstede above.

23. See, *inter alia*, R. N. Bellah, *Tokugawa Religion: The Values of Pre-Industrial Japan* (The Free Press:1957); I. Munakata, 'The Distinctive Features of Japanese Development: Basic Cultural Patterns and Politico-Economic Processes', in Berger and Hsiao, op. cit. pp.155–78; Y. Murakami, '*Ie* Society as a Pattern of Civilization', *Journal of Japanese Studies*, Vol.10, No.2 (1984), pp.281–363; Y. Murakami, 'Technology in Transition: Two Perspectives on Industrial Policy', in H. Patrick (ed.), *Japan's High-Technology Industries: Lessons and Limitations of Industrial Policy* (University of Washington Press:1986), pp.211–41; C. Nakane, *Japanese Society* (Penguin:1973).

24. Munakata, op. cit. p.161.

25. Bellah, op. cit.

26. R. Ketcham, *Individualism and Public Life* (Blackwell:1987).

27. See the excellent T. Elger and C. Smith (eds), *Global Japnization? The Transnational Transformation of the Labour Process* (Routledge:1994), for a range of cases, including from the US, Canada, UK, Sweden, Italy, Australia, Brazil. These question the universalizable content of many working practices.

28. Owing to the shortcomings inherent in this approach, one commentator has gone as far to say that cultural explanations of Japan's industrial prowess based on specifically Japanese traditions are 'nonsensical' since they amount to no more than saying that 'the Japanese are successful because they are Japanese' [W. M. Fruin, *The Japanese Enterprise System: Competitive Strategies and Cooperative Structures* (OUP:1994), p.2]. Fruin's judgement is surely accurate in so far as he here has in mind those studies that seek to locate Japan's post-war accumulation record in *pre*-industrial values whose impact is ultimately unquantifiable: the timing of Japan's take-off amidst ideological and institutional upheaval, and the extent to which it relied on high levels of quantifiable human and physical capital formation, do indeed make such theories untenable.

29. See Berger, Berger and Hsiao, Khan, Redding, op. cit.

30. The subtitle of Morishima's influential book *Why Has Japan Succeeded?*, for example, is *Western Technology and the Japanese Ethos* [M. Morishima, (CUP:1992)] and Tai (op. cit. p.26) notes the importance of Western technology to Asian success by admitting that the Orient would not have been able to industrialize in the first place unless it had obtained the

means to do so from the West via technology transfer.

31. Khan, op. cit. p.122.
32. Berger, Berger and Hsiao, Hung-Chao, Khan, Redding, op. cit.
33. Berger, op. cit. p.170.
34. Ibid. p.166.
35. See A. Whitehill, *Japanese Management* (Routledge:1991).
36. This sort of approach is adopted by, *inter alia*, R. Whitely, *European Business Systems* (Sage:1992); M. Maurice, F. Sellier, and J.-J. Silvestre, *The Social Foundations of Indstrial Power* (MIT Press:1986).
37. K. Fukuda, 'Japanese Companies in China: Problems of HRM', *Journal of Far Eastern Business*, Vol.1, No.4 (1995), pp.48–62.
38. L. Moore and P. Jennings (eds), *Human Resource Management on the Pacific Rim: Institutions, Practices and Attitudes* (de Gruyter:1995).
39. S. Frenkel (ed), *Organized Labor in the Asia-Pacific Region: A Comparative Study of Trade Unionism in Nine Countries* (ILR Press:1993).
40. B. Wilkinson, *Labour and Industry in the Asia-Pacific: Lessons From Newly-Industrialized Countries* (de Gruyter:1994).
41. A. Weber, *Theory of the Location of Industries* (Chicago University Press:1909, republished 1929).
42. R. Vernon, 'International Investment and International Trade in the Product Cycle', *Quarterly Journal of Economics*, Vol.80 (1966), pp.190–207; R. Vernon, 'The Product Life Cycle Hypothesis in A New Industrial Environment', *Oxford Economic Papers*, Vol.41, No.4 (1979), pp.255–67; S. Hirsch, *Location of Industry and International Competitiveness* (Clarendon Press:1967); B. Dankbaar, 'Maturity and Relocation in the Car Industry', *Development and Change*, Vol.15 (1984), pp.223–50.
43. R. Reich, *Work of Nations* (Simon and Schuster: 1993).
44. See, *inter alia*, F. Deyo, *Beneath the Miracle: Labor Subordination in the New Asian Industrialism* (University of California Press:1989); Wilkinson, op. cit.; Frenkel, op. cit.; More and Jennings, op. cit.; S. Deery and R. Mitchell, *Labour Law and Industrial Relations in Asia* (Longman Cheshire:1993); M. Rothman, D. Briscoe and R. Nacamulli (eds), *Industrial Relations Around the World: Labor Relations For Multinational Companies* (de Gruyter:1992).
45. Moore and Jennings, op. cit.
46. Ibid.
47. M. Warner, 'Managing Human Resources in East Asia', *International Journal of Human Resource Management*, Vol.6, No.1 (1995), pp.177–80.
48. M. Warner, *The Management of Human Resources in Chinese Industry* (St. Martin's Press:1995)
49. D. Kaple, *Dream of A Red Factory: The Legacy of High Stalinism in China* (Oxford University Press:1994).
50. J. Child, *Management in China During the Age of Reform* (Cambridge University Press:1994).
51. Crothall, op. cit.
52. Ibid.; Warner, op. cit.
53. The following is taken from Wilkinson, op. cit.
54. Ibid.
55. Ibid. p.178.
56. See, *inter alia*, R. Freeman and J. Medoff, *What Do Unions Do?* (Basic Books:1984); P. Nolan, 'Walking on Water? Performance and Industrial Relations Under Thatcher', *Industrial Relations Journal*, Vol. 20, No.2 (1989), pp.81–92; P. Nolan and K. O'Donnell, 'Industrial Relations and Productivity', in P. Edwards (ed), *Industrial Relations: Theory and Practice in Britain* (Blackwell:1995), pp.397–433; World Development Report, *Workers in An Internationalising World* (1995).
57. One could possibly argue that we have constructed a false or obsolete argument. After all, it could be noted many economies based on such labour market characteristics are in crisis. This is the debate between 'flexibility' and 'rigidity' (presented in European terms as 'Eurosclerosis'). Yet moves towards removing such 'rigidities' (which are often really a safety net of labour provision), under the seductive guise of 'flexibility', needs to be thought through. For example, it means that the proportion of those in permanent, full time, salaried jobs will decrease, with increases in part time, temporary, contract jobs. In the UK, the effects of this include employers taking on people at below 'living wages' and relying on the state

to 'top up' pay (with 'in-work benefits'). The result of this is the transfer of responsibility for maintaining incomes of much of the population from private firms to the public purse. At the same time, the conditions for 'private pensions' (a 'hot' topic in the UK and European countries) are no longer in place, with an increasing fall back on the state again.

58. The following is based on Frenkel, op. cit.; Deery and Mitchell, op. cit.
59. Child, 1994, op. cit.
60. Wilkinson, op. cit.
61. Ibid.
62. Ibid.
63. P. Krugman quoted in P. Montagon, 'Both Perspiration and Inspiration', *Financial Times Singapore Survey*, 8 February (1996), p.II.
64. W. Barnes, 'Labour: Schooled in Skills Shortage', *Financial Times Thailand Survey*, 14 December (1995), p.IV.
65. R. Dore, *British Factory–Japanese Factory: The Origins of National Diversity in Industrial Relations* (Allen and Unwin:1974).
66. T. Elger and C. Smith, 'Global Japanization? Convergence and Competition in the Organization of the Labour Process', in Elger and Smith, op. cit., pp.31–59.
67. Ibid. p.33.
68. Ibid.

The Political Economy of Greater China

TSANG SHU-KI

CHINA, GREATER CHINA AND THE ASIA PACIFIC REGION

Since 1979, China has made tremendous progress in its economic reform, which has two major aspects: the internal restructuring of the economy, and the opening up of the economy to external trade and foreign investment. It is of course the latter aspect, the open policy, which has generated the most significant direct impact on the economies outside China, particularly its neighbours in the Asia Pacific region. China's total trade (valued in US$) increased by 848.2 per cent in 1978–93, while the total values of contracted foreign funds and actual utilization of foreign funds (both including borrowing) amounted to US$314.373 billion and US$137.79 billion respectively in 1979–93.[1]

In such a process, Hong Kong and Taiwan have been most deeply involved, so much so that the term 'Greater China' has been coined to describe the rapidly growing triangular linkages among the three economies. Tables 1 and 2 show the relative importance of Hong Kong and Taiwan to China's external economics. One point to note is that the trade and investment figures definitely understate the importance of Taiwan, as direct trade with China is still not officially allowed by the Taiwanese authorities, although indirect trade through Hong Kong has been thriving. Moreover, for both trade and investment, it is widely believed that the Hong Kong statistics actually include major Taiwan interests, which use Hong Kong as a vehicle for economic, as well as political, expediency. We shall have more to say on this later. In any case, the key position of Hong Kong and Taiwan in China's external economic exchanges is clearly borne out in the two tables.[2] At the same time, there is little doubt that China is the locomotive in that emerging economic entity dubbed Greater China, given its huge size and potential. So a study of their inter-relations will yield insights on how China's open policy is generating impacts on its neighbours, especially the close ones, in the region.

PHENOMENAL GROWTH MOMENTUM IN GREATER CHINA

All the three economies of Greater China – mainland China, Taiwan and Hong Kong – share one common feature, that is very high growth momentum. Taiwan and Hong Kong have of course been part of the 'East Asian miracle'. In the period 1970–93, the Taiwan economy has grown

Tsang Shu-ki, Hong Kong Baptist University

more than six times, yielding an average annual real growth rate of 8.6 per cent.[3] At a higher level of development, Hong Kong's record is also impressive, average annual growth rate in 1970–93 having been 7.4 per cent.[4] According to official statistics, in 1992, per capita GDP in Hong Kong reached US$16,480 (8th in the world), while per capita GNP in Taiwan was US$10,202 (25th in the world). Taiwan's nominal GNP reached US$244.2 billion in 1994, making it the 20th largest economy in the world.[5]

TABLE 1

COMPOSITION OF CHINA'S DIRECT TRADE WITH THE ASIA PACIFIC REGION

%	1978		1986		1992	
	Exports	Imports	Exports	Imports	Exports	Imports
USA	2.8	6.6	8.4	10.9	10.1	10.9
Asia Pacific:	49.4	31.7	53.4	45.1	66.2	58.3
Japan	17.6	28.4	16.2	28.8	13.7	16.7
NIEs:	28.5	1.1	35.1	14.2	49.9	37.0
Hong Kong	26.0	0.7	31.2	12.9	43.9	25.1
Taiwan					0.8	7.2
S.Korea					2.9	3.2
Singapore	2.5	0.4	3.9	1.3	2.4	1.5
ASEAN:	3.3	2.2	2.1	2.1	2.6	4.6
Indonesia			0.5	0.7	0.6	1.9
Malaysia	1.7	1.0	0.6	0.4	0.8	1.0
Philippines	0.9	0.5	0.5	0.3	0.2	0.2
Thailand	0.7	0.7	0.5	0.7	1.0	0.5

Source: IMF, *Direction of Trade Statistics.*

TABLE 2

FOREIGN DIRECT INVESTMENTS IN CHINA, 1979–93

	No. of foreign invested companies	%	Registered capital (US$bn)	%
Hong Kong	108,914	63.8	103.9	72.7
Taiwan	20,612	12.3	13.2	9.3
USA	11,554	6.9	8.2	5.7
Japan	7,096	4.2	5.2	3.6
Macau	4,116	2.5	4.1	2.9
Singapore	3037	1.8	3.3	2.3
S.Korea	2321	1.4	1.3	0.9
Canada	1595	0.9	1.0	0.7
Thailand	1361	0.8	1.6	1.1
Australia	1269	0.8	1.0	0.7
Total	167,507	100.0	142.9	100.0

Source: *Jingji Yanjiu Cankao*, 12 October 1994.

Mainland China is another story. Cynics may say that it 'joined the modern world' only in 1978. Despite hiccups in politics and the economic reform in the past 14 years, annual real growth in 1979–93 averaged 9.3 per cent.[6] Moreover, unlike in the 1980s, when growth was propelled by light industries and outward processing, growth in the 1990s is increasingly infrastructure-led and driven by heavy industries. Many informed economists would now agree that because of the much stronger forward and backward linkage effects, an annual growth rate of ten per cent is sustainable for the coming decade, barring of course political turmoil.[7]

In 1992, at the then official exchange rate of 5.7 yuan per US$, China's per capita GNP (about US$370) was ridiculously low. Both the IMF and the World Bank do not believe this to be accurate. Their estimates, based on the so called PPP (purchasing power parity) adjustment methods, push the figure up by four to six times. Because of China's huge population, being the world's largest at over 1.1 billion, the absolute size of the Chinese economy in 1990 was ranked the world's second by the World Bank (after the US),[8] and third by the IMF (after the US and Japan).[9]

If double-digit growth were to be sustained, China might overtake the United States as the world's largest economy around the year 2010 – a haunting vision that has attracted much popular attention lately. The British weekly journal *The Economist* must be given credit for highlighting such a possibility as early as October 1992. Based on the PPP-adjusted regression approximation of the World Bank, which puts China's per-capita GDP at US$2,040.0 for 1991,[10] Hong Kong's GDP was about four per cent of China's GNP, and Taiwan's GNP about 9 per cent. The latter's estimated real growth rates for the coming decade, at 5–7 per cent, will be substantially lower than China's, but still comfortably higher than the projected 3 per cent (or less) of that of the United States. So the combined economic size of Greater China could surpass the US economy in 10–12 years' time, if the methodology of PPP-based estimates is accepted.

Nevertheless, it must be noted that by the year 2010 China's total population would be about five times that of the US, compared with 4.5 times in 1992, taking into account demographic trends. In other words, even as mainland China finds satisfaction in becoming the largest economy on earth, its per capita GNP, adjusted for PPP considerations, would still only be one-fifth of the US. China should in no sense be regarded as a 'superpower', unless of course if the matter is looked at from a geo-political perspective. Sitting on the largest resource bundle of the world, the yet unreformed authoritarian rulers in Beijing could do things that a President or a Prime Minister in the West could not do. If the basic problems of economic survival and poverty are solved, the huge population – one-fifth of mankind – might also be a political asset rather than liability, not to mention the power of its cultural links with the overseas Chinese, many of whom would feel proud of an increasingly powerful motherland.

RAPID ECONOMIC INTEGRATION

The second prominent feature of Greater China as an economic entity is the rapid pace of intra-regional 'integration'. Integration is at a more advanced stage between China and Hong Kong than between China and Taiwan. The opening of China has dramatically changed Hong Kong's industrial structure. A massive process of relocating manufacturing plants from Hong Kong to China has taken place. Over three million employees in the Guangdong province of China are reportedly working directly or indirectly for Hong Kong, compared with the total work force of about three million in the territory itself. Hong Kong now handles the traffic of over half of China's external trade, and its container port at Kwai Chung is one of the busiest in the world. Hong Kong is China's largest 'outside investor',[11] and China is Hong Kong's second largest. While Hong Kong's share in China's total contracted foreign investment is over 60 per cent, China's investment in Hong Kong is estimated to be about US$20 billion, second only to that of Britain.[12] According to estimates by the economists of the Hang Seng Bank in Hong Kong, 25.7 per cent of Hong Kong's GDP in 1990 was attributable to 'the China factor'. This compares with 5.3 per cent in 1980.[13] The ratio must now be rising. It is not easy to find a successful businessperson in Hong Kong who has no investments in China.

In contrast, Taiwan has been much more guarded as far as economic integration is concerned, fearing that there would be serious political repercussions. Indirect trade between Mainland China and Taiwan grew 110 times in 1979–93, at an average annual rate of 55 per cent.[14] It must be remembered that the initial base, at about US$78 million in 1979, was extremely small. In 1994, Taiwan's indirect trade with China through Hong Kong amounted to US$9.8095 billion, or 5.5 per cent of its global trade (see Table 3). Such a figure is however widely regarded as understating the real volume. Trade with Hong Kong in the same year, on the basis of Taiwan statistics, amounted to US$22.7985 billion, or 12.8 per cent of Taiwan's global trade. The actual volume of trade with China is likely to lie between these two sets of figures because some exports from Taiwan, reportedly heading for Hong Kong (without being re-exported to the mainland), eventually go to China after various forms of 'transhipment' or 'transitting' in Hong Kong or even totally by-passing Hong Kong. These would not go into the 'indirect trade' statistics as reflected by re-exports through Hong Kong. Economists have called such phenomena variously 'transshipment', 'transitting', 'direct trade' or 'illegal trade'.[15] Moreover, there is also another (probably small) amount of 'illegal trade', notably trade on ships off the coast of the Fujian Province in China or routed through South Korea and Ryukyu Islands.[16] In March 1995, Hong Kong for the first time overtook the United States as Taiwan's largest export outlet, accounting for 24 per cent of the total and edging out the 23.3 per cent of the US. According to the Finance Ministry, some 60 per cent of the total exports to Hong Kong (as reported in Table 3) were bound for mainland China, especially electronic parts and raw materials.[17]

TABLE 3
TAIWAN'S TRADE WITH CHINA AND HONG KONG
(US$m)

	Indirect Trade via HK		Total trade with HK	
	Exports to China	Imports to China	Exports to HK	Imports from HK
1979	21.5	56.3	1140.1 (7.08)	205.5 (1.39)
1980	235.0	76.2	1550.6 (7.83)	249.9 (1.27)
1981	384.2	75.2	1835.9 (8.38)	299.7 (1.46)
1982	194.5	84.0	1563.2 (7.04)	300.4 (1.63)
1983	157.8	89.9	1642.4 (6.54)	298.2 (1.47)
1984	425.5	127.8	2086.3 (6.85)	371.1 (1.69)
1985	986.8	115.9	2539.7 (8.26)	319.7 (1.59)
1986	811.3	144.2	2921.3 (7.32)	378.7 (1.56)
1987	1226.5	288.9	4123.3 (7.68)	753.8 (2.15)
1988	2242.2	478.7	5587.1 (9.21)	1922.1 (3.87)
1989	2896.5	586.9	7042.3 (10.61)	2205.2 (4.26)
1990	3278.3	765.4	8556.2 (12.75)	1445.9 (2.64)
1991	4667.2	1125.9	12430.5 (16.30)	1946.8 (3.10)
1992	6287.9	1119.0	15415.0 (18.92)	1781.4 (2.48)
1993	7585.4	1103.6	18444.3 (21.70)	1728.6 (2.24)
1994	8517.2	1292.3	21265.9 (22.85)	1532.6 (1.80)

Note: The figures in parenthesis represent the percentage of Hong Kong in Taiwan's trade.

Sources: 'Taiwan Economic Statistics', *Industry of Free China*; Chi Schive. 'Taiwan's Economic Restructuring in the 1980s and its New Role in the Asian Pacific', *Industry of Free China*, August 1994, pp.29–50.

In testimony to the legislature in April 1995, Economics Minister P.K. Chiang revealed that Taiwan's trade surplus with Hong Kong amounted to US$17.5 billion (presumably for the year of 1994), 60–70 per cent of which were re-exported to China. If the economic exchanges between China and Taiwan were halted, he reckoned that 15 per cent of Taiwan's exports would be affected and the annual loss could be as high as US$12 billion.[18] Even just looking at Taiwan's indirect trade with China through Hong Kong, its surplus with China was already US$6.481 billion in 1993, or 83 per cent of its total trade surplus of the year.[19] On the other hand, Taiwan is now the

second largest investor in China, accounting for 12.3 per cent of the number
of FICs and 9.3 per cent of the total registered capital at the end of 1993.[20]
While direct Chinese investment in Taiwan is politically non-existent,
mainland Chinese capital has been entering Taiwan through companies
registered in Hong Kong.

The differences between Hong Kong's and Taiwan's linkages with
mainland China reflect the varied modes of politics within Greater China.
Hong Kong is too small, economically as well as politically, to put up serious
resistance to the forces of market integration. The Hong Kong
administration, given its admiration for free market economics in the form
of 'positive non-interventionism', has also been ill-equipped to deal with any
macro-structural changes of such proportions. The Taiwanese government is
much more interventionist. Moreover, its economic stance towards China is
still highly influenced by politics, particularly its fear that economic
integration may undermine its bargaining power in the negotiations about
unification or its bid to become independent, at least in a *de facto* sense. In
any case, the magnetic effect of China on Taiwan is still very strong. The
following quote of Vincent C. Siew, the former Chairman of Taiwan's
Council for Economic Planning and Development (and later the Chairman
of its Mainland Affairs Committee), is self-explanatory:

> In fact, the rapid growth of trade across the Straits (of Taiwan) has
> become one of the most important factors behind the steady growth of
> the Taiwan economy in very recent years. From a long-term point of
> view, the further integration of the two economies is a trend that
> would be difficult to thwart. The important question for Taiwan,
> therefore, is how to face up to this situation, grasp the initiative, strive
> for mutually beneficial development, and secure a position of
> economic leadership.'[21]

PROBLEMS AND PROSPECTS:
THE CONTRADICTIONS BETWEEN ECONOMICS AND POLITICS

The economic prospects look relatively bright for Greater China if
mainland China, obviously the locomotive of the three entities, functions
well. It should be noted that both Hong Kong and Taiwan were running into
some kind of economic troubles before 'connecting' to China in the late
1970s and the first half of 1980s respectively, as their mode of 'labour-
intensive, export-oriented growth' faced domestic constraints in the form of
rising costs as well as external market restrictions. Technological upgrading
and market diversification seemed to be the unavoidable solutions.
Unexpectedly, the China link offered an 'easy' way out, 'short-circuiting'
the rapidly approaching difficulties. This was more so for Hong Kong than
for Taiwan. Amidst the short-term bonanza, though, some longer-term side
effects, which are not necessarily benign in nature, have emerged. To deal
with them effectively, vision and commitment on the part of both the

government and the private sector, is required.

If the political dimension is taken into consideration, the situation becomes more complicated. Even Hong Kong, which on the whole has relatively little bargaining power vis-à-vis China, has not been spared of the transition politics of 1997. On the other hand, a more powerful Taiwan, given the historical twists and turns in the past century and the present drive towards *de jure* or *de facto* independence by a minority, but vocal, sector of the population, is caught in a tug-of-war between contrasting forces of politics and economics. Whether economic rationality will prevail in the end is a contentious point.

Hong Kong

For Hong Kong, the painful process of pondering in the second half of 1970s was cut short as the opening of China presented an unprecedented opportunity to lower costs, even without technological upgrading or market diversification for the territory's manufacturing industries. With the massive relocation of factories and plants to Southern China, Hong Kong could concentrate on services. Hence a rapid process of 'structural transformation' of Hong Kong towards a 'service economy' has unfolded. Some would of course call this 'de-industrialization'. The prime evidence is the rapid shrinking of the local manufacturing work force. At the end of 1984, the manufacturing sector employed 904,709 workers. The total number had been halved by 1994 and fell below 400,000 in 1995 (see Table 4). That the manufacturing work force of an economy could be trimmed by 50 per cent within ten years must be one of the records in world economic history. In the mean time, major service sectors have had their employment doubled. The ease with which employees have switched across sectors appears to be a testimony to the famous flexibility of the Hong Kong economy.

Critics would however argue that it reflects rather poorly on the skill level in the major economic sectors. The superficial labour mobility runs counter to the trend of productivity enhancement, usually accompanied by specialization, professionalization, and accumulation of expertise. As I have argued elsewhere, the so called 'structural transformation' of the Hong Kong economy is more a case of regional reallocation of resources as a result of China's open policy, which has enabled both sides to reap huge short-term profits. Nevertheless, in so far as such gains from static advantages release pressure for climbing the technological ladder and nurturing long-term competitive capabilities, far-sightedness is required for ensuring lasting prosperity and stability.[22]

By 1995, the territory had the first glimpse of the potential problems of rapid de-industrialization, as sagging demands in the service sectors undermined their ability to absorb switched and newly generated labour supply, resulting in a ten-year high unemployment rate of 3.5 per cent for June to August. Although cyclical factors have certainly been an important factor, some deep-seated problems, such as aggravating income inequality and structural mismatch between jobs and skills, have also been revealed.

TABLE 4
EMPLOYMENT BY SECTOR IN HONG KONG

	1984	1993	March 1995
Manufacturing	904,709	483,628	395,437
Construction sites	67,732	55,852	64,093
Wholesale, retail, import-export trade, hotels, restaurants	548,594	948,881	1,015,128
Finance, insurance, real estate, business services	165,032	338,093	361,328

Note: The numbers are period-end figures.

Source: *Report of Employment, Vacancies, and Payroll Statistics*, Hong Kong Government.

As far as the 1997 transition is concerned, China may relish an increase or reduction in the economic importance of Hong Kong, in the light of the unfolding political developments of 'one country, two systems', on top of natural changes in its dependence on the territory in the course of its economic reform. The row with Britain since October 1992, when Hong Kong Governor Chris Patten initiated electoral reforms without China's consent, has heightened political tension. China already vowed to disband in 1997 the territory's legislature and re-establish one according to the Basic Law (the mini-constitution governing the post-1997 system). So far, though, the impact of the political row on the Hong Kong economy has been quite mild in terms of growth and investment. Indeed, international and domestic enthusiasm about China after the Deng whirlwind of 1992 produced a property and stock market boom in 1993–94. It looks likely that the Hong Kong economy can weather the political storms of 1997, unless events in China take a totally unexpected turn.

Looking ahead, a thoroughly capitalistic China probably would enhance Hong Kong's role. Alternatively, a suspicious China, still troubled by internal contradictions and anxious about Britain's motives in its twilight years in the colony as well as the behaviour of 'internationally-linked' anti-China 'democrats' around and beyond 1997, could resort to a strategy of 'diversion', transferring 'portions of prosperity' northwards to Southern China – a sphere more easily controlled. One key leverage is to ensure that crucial infrastructure or markets be located in the Pearl River Delta rather than in Hong Kong. A metaphor is that Hong Kong should continue to be the magical goose that lays golden eggs, but don't let it become too fat, lest it may be stolen. (Or don't let its ego expand too much, otherwise it will walk or fly away.) However, some would regard such a prediction as purely speculative because Beijing does not have that degree of strategic control in a decentralized era. Economic rationality would also rule out that course of action.[23]

The de-industrialization of Hong Kong has been phenomenal. Such a process can be termed 'Manhattanization', under which tertiary services rapidly dominates the economy. The trend has been largely caused by the China factor. In the longer run, there is however doubt whether Hong Kong's importance to China can be maintained. Hong Kong has so far served China well in three major areas, namely as its port, marketing outlet, and financier. It appears that Hong Kong may see a decline in its relative importance in all three roles in the future, as China's economic strength rises and its direct contact with the outside world deepens.

Some commentators have emphasized the fact that Hong Kong's importance as a trade intermediary actually increased in the 1980s even as China opened herself to the world. Various reasons based on the theory of economic intermediation are invoked. The usefulness of Hong Kong stems from its ability to provide services that would reduce the transaction costs for foreigners in doing business with China, because of the territory's geographical proximity and cultural affinity to China as well as its 'first-mover' advantages, such as accumulated experience and economies of scale.[24] Interesting as such an analysis is, to extrapolate it without careful consideration of changing dynamics would be shaky logic. This explanation has neglected the technical reason that China's transportation and communications facilities had not been able to catch up with its rapidly expanding volume of external trade. Therefore, it had no choice but to route a good deal of trade through Hong Kong, with all the related service provisions. China has now entered into a period of vast infrastructural build-up, highlighted by all the ambitious plans for airports, ports, railways and highways. Hence 'diversion' (or some would say 'reversion') of a significant portion of external economic exchanges may proceed. On the other hand Shanghai, Guangzhou, Shenzhen and Zhuhai all aspire to be 'international financial centres', aiming in taking at least some businesses which might otherwise be done in Hong Kong.

This does not mean that Hong Kong will lose all its major functions. These developments however point to the possibility that Hong Kong may get a smaller share of the pie in the future. Without a viable industrial base, the territory would have to undergo further 'structural transformation' to keep ahead of other competing cities. Consequently, Hong Kong could be pushed into a peculiar mode of specialization, and only services which show characteristics of a very 'high-risk, high-returns trade-off' might find it viable to be locally based. The trouble is that these activities would push up inflation because their cost and benefit calculations are quite different from manufacturing or even normal services. Moreover, only a limited proportion of the territory's population can engage profitably in these activities. Persistent unemployment may then emerge as a headache. Ironically, then, Hong Kong will be even more 'Manhattanized', as de-industrialization totalizes, financial wizardry dominates and the ugly reality of poverty in the midst of affluence comes to the surface. Hong Kong's income distribution is already the worst among those economies with comparable per capita GDP or GNP.[25] It could further deteriorate under this scenario of forced 'Manhattanization'. A proactive remedial policy stance, especially at the redistributive level of fiscal and welfare measures, may be necessary to maintain basic economic and social balance.

Some will argue that the de-industrialization of Hong Kong is no worry at all. However such a comment is misleading, because unlike some cities Hong Kong will be a *separate* economic system under Chinese sovereignty, according to the Sino-British Joint Declaration and the Basic Law. The post-1997 Hong Kong Special Administrative Region (SAR) will continue to issue an independent currency, maintain its fiscal autonomy, and determine its own migration policy. Hong Kong residents will not be able to migrate to Guangdong in the same way that US citizens move from New York to California. Hence, any local structural unemployment cannot be solved by a transfer of manpower to the north. If there is a fiscal or a balance-of-payments crisis in Hong Kong, Beijing is not supposed to extend rescue measures to the territory directly. In short, the Hong Kong economy cannot be *fully* integrated into China's because there will not be totally free flows of monetary, fiscal and human resources, under the rule of 'one country, two systems'. The Hong Kong economy must maintain a degree of *coherence* which is much higher than any metropolitan city in a national economy. Coherence would imply a better balance between industry and service, prosperity and equity.

Taiwan

Compared with Hong Kong, Taiwan has been much more activist in shaping its own economic future. It has embarked on a route of technological upgrading and market diversification, dubbed 'second-stage export orientation' (IS2), with some success. In 1971–80, exports of textile, leather and paper products represented 44 per cent of Taiwan's total manufactured exports, while exports of machinery and apparatus accounted for 22 per cent. In 1991–92, the former ratio fell to 25 per cent as the latter rose to 36 per cent. Taiwan has also been building its own cars and ships, and has its own oil refineries and chemical plants.

Yet economic upgrading in Taiwan has not been implemented with the type of determination and coordination witnessed in, say, Japan, South Korea or Singapore. Since the early 1980s, the government has not undertaken any significant public investments, particularly in infrastructure. This has led to a 'deterioration of investment environment' as private investors were discouraged by the inadequacy of public facilities, including water and electricity supply and efficient transportation.[26] The uncertainty in the process of political liberalization which ended the Nationalist Party's monopoly has also been a contributing factor. In sharp contrast, the sluggishness in domestic demand has been mirrored in the huge trade surplus that has emerged. At US$83.6 billion by the end of 1993, Taiwan's foreign exchange reserve was the second largest in the world. Not surprisingly, such external imbalance has incurred the wrath of the US, which suffers from a large deficit in its trade with Taiwan.

Taiwan's economic connection to China began officially in November 1987 when indirect contact and trade were legally allowed and, to a number of commentators, this has been a mixed blessing. On the one hand, it has provided a golden opportunity for Taiwan to increase its trade competitiveness by lowering costs and yields new outlets for frustrated private entrepreneurs. So even high-ranking officials such as Vincent Siew admit that 'the rapid growth of trade across the Straits has become one of the most important factors behind the steady growth of the Taiwan economy in very recent years'. On the other hand, though, the China connection has been blamed for various problems including draining Taiwan's liquid funds in the early 1990s (so the stock market collapsed and the government found it difficult to sell bonds to finance its infrastructure projects), as well as leading to a 'hollowing out' of Taiwan's industries as investors shifted out of high-tech concerns and poured money into sweatshop factories in China, thus side-stepping the efforts to climb the technological ladder. One superficial indication of the latter phenomenon is that the share of manufacturing industries in GNP fell from over 40 per cent in the 1970s to 34.4 in 1990 and further dipped to 31.6 in 1993.[27]

In their popular versions, these allegations are in my opinion exaggerated. Mainland Chinese figures put the total stock of Taiwanese investment in the mainland at US$13.2 billion in 1979–93,[28] although the Taiwan authority thinks that it is higher, some US$15–20 billion by 1992. These figures are not large compared with the US$83.6 billion of official foreign exchange reserve at the end of 1993 or the size of Taiwan's GNP, at US$220.129 billion in 1993.[29] Taiwan cannot blame all its internal problems on the China connection.[30]

In the long run, of course, there can be a real danger. As we have noted, on PPP-adjusted estimates of the World Bank, Taiwan's GNP is about nine per cent of China's. A possibility exists that if Taiwan does not put its own house in order, it will be absorbed and assimilated into the Mainland economy. Then it will rise or fall with the latter. To be fair, the Taiwan government has been making responses. There is also a fear that increasing investment by Taiwanese entrepreneurs in China might replace domestic investment within Taiwan and lead to a negative impact on Taiwan's output.[31] In reaction, Taiwan launched a 'Six Year National Development Plan' in 1991 with heavy emphasis on infrastructure investments,[32] and in July 1993 it unveiled an 'Economic Revitalization Programme' that aimed to accelerate industrial upgrading and develop Taiwan into an 'Asia Pacific regional operations centre' (APROC), largely through the promotion of private investment. The official plan on the APROC was passed by the Executive Yuan in Taiwan in late December 1994.[33] The plan was however not entirely defensive in nature, as the setting up of the APROC would stand

Taiwan in good stead in benefitting from the possible windfalls of a China boom in the Asia Pacific region, albeit in a more broadly-based context. It was also a move to develop the tertiary sector in Taiwan and improve the overall economic structure.[34]

In 1995, the political relationship between China and Taiwan entered a new stage as the so-called 'eight-point statement' of peaceful unification by the Chinese President Jiang Zemin early in the year did not receive an enthusiastic response from Taiwanese President Lee Teng-hui. Moreover, Lee went on a spree of efforts to create 'international space', including an 'unofficial' trip to the US, which implied from Beijing's perspective a rather strong sense of striving towards independence, at least in a *de facto* sense. These developments, plus the problems between China and the US, resulted in rising tension across the Taiwan Strait, dramatized by military tests by China.

A key question is whether all these manoeuveres are a result of transitional politicking in both Taiwan (towards democratization of a presidential type) and China (towards the post-Deng era), which unfortunately becomes synchronized at this particular historical juncture, or stem from genuine, fundamentally unresolvable conflicts. Opinion surveys in Taiwan have never shown a support for independence much above 20 per cent. After the missile tests by China in the Taiwan Strait in July 1995, support fell to only 12 per cent, according to one poll.[35] Creating more 'international space' and bargaining chips is one thing, while independence is an entirely different matter. Therefore, an educated guess is that there is a chance for the tension to be reduced beyond the transitional process. Mainland China has in the meantime made effort to attract Taiwan's investors by stressing that their economic interests will be protected.

Mainland China

We will now look at the prospect of the locomotive, the Chinese economy. World opinion remains rather volatile, wavering between 'maximum bullishness' and outright pessimism. Nevertheless, most would agree on one thing: after the 'Deng whirlwind' of early 1992 and the 14th Party Congress in October 1992, there is little doubt that China is sincere in pushing forward market-oriented reforms.[36] Moreover, the growth pattern has changed into a infrastructure-led and heavy-industry-driven one, which requires huge amounts of capital. Given the shortage of capital in China, the country has to depend on external funding for its economic take-off. Indeed, in many of the medium-term and long-term development plans recently announced by the central as well as the local authorities, external funding is conspicuously emphasized, its planned share in total financing ranging from 25 to as high as 50 per cent.

Foreign investors seem to have responded favourably to these changes in China. Capital inflows into China since 1992 have broken all past records. The contracted amount of foreign direct investment (FDI) in 1992, at US$58.7 billion, exceeded the cumulative amount from 1979 to 1991 – a phenomenal leap by any standard. The surge remained unabated in 1993: contracted FDI rose by another astonishing 91.7 per cent over 1992, while the actual utilization of foreign capital, at US$ 38.96 billion, chalked up a growth rate of 102.9 per cent.[37]

This seems to be a promising start to China's plan to build a 'socialist market economy' which is open to the rest of the world. The basic driving force is simple: most people are now convinced that the Chinese economy has become more market-friendly and foreign-capital-friendly, and that the reform process has entered an irreversible phase, by design or by default, after the difficult years of 1989–91. To prove its emphasis on attracting external funds, China has reshaped its foreign-capital absorption policy. Previously, the policy was dominated by a regional orientation: investments in the coastal regions were given various favourable terms. Now, an industrial orientation has apparently taken over. The whole of the country is supposed to be open to foreign investment, while preferential treatments are to be guided by an industrial policy.

Three priority sectors have been identified: infrastructure, high-tech industries, and the tertiary sector.[38] These are bottlenecks that constrain the further development of the Chinese economy. On paper at least, foreign investors will now be able to invest in these priority sectors in any part of China, be it Hubei or Fujian, Heilongjiang or Qinghai, and receive similar preferential treatment. In any case, the net effect is that many spheres which were previously closed to, or restricted from, foreign investments are now in the process of opening up, including commerce, retail business, finance, insurance, inland transportation, air navigation, land and property development and consultancy. The question is whether foreign funds would be forthcoming on such a massive scale.

Regardless of the huge potential of the Chinese economy, there are obviously many serious problems: ranging from the ineffectiveness in macroeconomic control, cyclical overheating, and worsening income and regional disparities, to growing regionalism, peasant rebellion, rampant corruption, and voids in collective goals. Most of these problems stem from China's peculiar mode of gradual, but wrongly sequenced, reforms and has a lot to do with Deng's pragmatism, which may be instrumental in ensuring short-term success and avoiding major blunders, but which lacks the vision and force that can hold the country together and move it towards a common long-term goal. The wrong sequencing is not related to sectoral priority, on which China has generally got the order right (from rural reform to urban reform). Rather, it concerns the alignment of microeconomic versus macroeconomic reforms. It must be remembered that the economic reform launched in 1979 was a attempt to salvage credibility and legitimacy for the Party, which had been badly shaken in the Cultural Revolution. Hence, the key strategy has been 'to decentralize power and to provide material incentive' (*fangchuan rangli*) to farmers, local authorities and enterprises to pacify them and to raise their living standard quickly.[39] In contrast, the need to build effective macroeconomic (fiscal and monetary) control and redistributive mechanisms, which even the most capitalist economy cannot do without, has largely been neglected, at least up to the very recent time.[40]

So a situation of 'economic warlordism' (*zhuhou jingji*) is being formed, under which parties of newly formed or vested interests vie for more concessions from the central government but resist its command. The central government finds itself caught in a vicious circle of administrative decentralization and fiscal decline. Worst of all, since any economic boom has been, on the surface at least, the result of decentralization, the only contribution of the central government is perceived to be essentially negative in nature – that is, by letting go its power. In the extreme, Beijing could be viewed as an increasingly irrelevant obstacle.[41]

China has not quite reached that stage yet. Moreover, the comprehensive reform package launched by the Third Plenum of the Fourteenth Central Committee of the Chinese Communist Party in November 1993 was clearly an attempt to revamp the central fiscal and monetary mechanisms that could supervise the rapidly evolving 'socialist market economy' before the total loss of control became a real danger. The top leaders, particularly Zhu Rongji and Jiang Zemin, have shown considerable courage and political skill in combining a 'stop–go' approach in macroeconomic adjustment with a relatively bold attempt at reforms that do not unduly infringe upon local interests. Of course, tough negotiations between Beijing and the local authorities are inevitable. In any case, packages that aimed at quickening the pace of reforms in banking and finance, foreign trade, foreign exchange, and the investment management systems were unveiled in 1994, although apparently they did not constitute the 'big bang' type of rapid liberalization experimented with in Russia and Eastern Europe. On the whole, the reforms have been quite successful, with the exception of the banking reform which has been hindered by the slow progress in the revamping of the state-owned industrial sector.[42]

The biggest uncertainty of all for mainland China is of course the question of political succession, when Deng Xiaoping finally passes away. In the absence of a paramount leader with historical charisma, the 'doomsday scenario' reads like a horror story in which the economic warlords gang up with the regional military authorities who have themselves become overly commercialized, the poor provinces fight against the coastal rich, peasant rebellions flare up; all these are watched helplessly by a weak and divided Beijing. At the same time refugees flood into Hong Kong, Taiwan, and the rest of the world, generating a 'yellow peril' of an unprecedented kind.

No one can rule out the possibility of such a scenario. However, as the saying goes, although everything is possible, only some are probable. While it might not be plain sailing for China in the post-Deng era, an intelligent guess is that a collective leadership could somehow 'muddle through'. A key factor is that the so called 'warlords' and the various parties of vested interests and non-interests in China now are basically fighting *not* for survival, but for a *better* life. Moreover, there are no fundamental ideological, ethnic or religious divisions among them. In other words, the pressure for them to act compulsively or desperately should not be unduly high. High growth rates are therefore the best buffer against political disintegration, and even cautious projections would grant China an annual average GDP expansion rate of 8–9 per cent in the coming decade, barring of course major economic warfare with the West led by the United States. This is not say that localized disturbances in some of the poorer regions and various forms of social dissent would not take place. But they are probably containable.

EXTERNAL CONSTRAINTS VERSUS INTERNAL DYNAMISM

If the above diagnosis and projections about the three members of Greater China are plausible assumptions to work on, we can proceed to discuss the internal and external dynamics of the further development of the economic circle. One important question is this: what is the prime source of growth for Greater China? Taiwan and Hong Kong have basically been export-driven in their phenomenal growth in the past, but could Greater China as a whole also be export-driven in the future? Alternatively, will 'domestic demand' within the economic circle itself be the major driving force?

So far, the tremendous increase in trade within Greater China has largely been the result of outward processing, from Hong Kong and Taiwan to mainland China, rather than that of intra-circle absorption, so that the activities have been dominated by the trade in intermediate goods. The case of Hong Kong is as clear as it is dramatic, as shown in Table 5. China's share in Hong Kong's domestic exports, re-exports and imports have all shown significant increases. However, adjusted for the outward processing activities that Hong Kong has transferred to southern China, Hong Kong's dependence on the US as the major end-user market for its goods has changed little in the past decade. While Hong Kong has carved a bigger share of the Chinese market, its imports from China now represent a smaller proportion than a decade ago.

TABLE 5
IMPORTANCE OF CHINA AND THE USA TO HONG KONG'S EXTERNAL TRADE (%)

	1981		1994		1994 (adjusted)	
	China	USA	China	USA	China	USA
Domestic exports	3.6	36.3	26.5	27.6	9.3	34.1
Re-exports to	19.3	11.5	33.9	22.2	22.5	26.0
Imports	21.3	10.4	37.4	7.1	12.6	10.0
Re-exports from	30.7	9.7	57.6	4.6	23.5	8.3

Note: Last columns are adjusted for outward processing activities. The adjustment is performed by netting out the 'estimated value involving outward processing in China' from the total trade figure and the trade amount with China. Such adjustment is possible only for figures after 1989, when the Hong Kong government first published the outward processing figures.

Source: Hong Kong Monthly Digest of Statistics, Hong Kong Government.

Statistical limitations do not allow similar direct adjustments for Taiwan's trade figures. But superficial inspection suggests that the same phenomenon has occurred. While the share of exports to the US fell from 45.1 per cent in 1983 to 27.7 in 1993, the proportion of exports to Hong Kong rose from 6.5 per cent to 21.7 in the same time period. As said above, Hong Kong overtook the US in export share in March 1995. However, such superficial statistics are deceptive. Much of the exports (60 to 70 per cent) to Hong Kong enter mainland China for processing and are then re-exported, with a significant portion going to the US.

The US side of the story seems to confirm this analysis. A commentary released by the United States Information Service (USIS) in Hong Kong presented figures as shown in Table 6 and admit that:

> when looked at since 1987, the US trade deficit with Greater China rose by only five percent in the entire five year period through 1992. Although the deficit with the PRC climbed by some US$15 billion during 1987–92, the US trade deficit shrank about US$14 billion with Hong Kong and Taiwan combined during the same period, giving rise to the belief that (the) two dragons had managed to shift their surpluses to the PRC.

TABLE 6
US TRADE BALANCE WITH GREATER CHINA (US$bn)

	1987	1990	1991	1992
P.R. China	-2.7	-10.3	-12.7	-18.2
Taiwan	-17.6	-11.4	-9.8	-9.4
Hong Kong	-27.0	-24.4	-23.7	-28.3

Source: 'Greater China Trade with the United States, 1987-92', *Economic Policy Backgrounder*, USIS, Hong Kong, 23 March 1993.

To be fair, moreover, the fact that US's deficit with Greater China as a whole rose only five per cent is a testimony that the latter has also imported a great deal from the US.

As to the future, the signs are conflicting. On the one hand, a report by the World Bank comes up with the optimistic conclusion[43] that there is still decent room for China to expand its exports without rapid upgrading of products, as 'there remains substantial scope for OECD markets to absorb developing country exports of manufacture', at least up to 1998, barring major disasters like the collapse of the Uruguay Round of the GATT talks or the non-renewal of China's MFN status by the US (both of which did not materialize). In the longer run, though, the constraints would become increasingly severe, and it is important that there be an upgrading of products and diversification of markets. One danger for Greater China is that since money is easily earned without much effort in upgrading and diversification, both governments and entrepreneurs may become complacent.[44] This brings us back to the issue of 'hollowing out'.

On the other hand, even an upgrading of products is no guarantee for peace and prosperity on the international trade front. The US–Japan trade conflict is a classic lesson. As for Greater China, much hope has been pinned on its internal dynamism and the fact the China is potentially the most lucrative market in the world. To some commentators, there is no intrinsic reason why China should be externally oriented to such a high degree. In 1992, for example, the ratio of external trade to GNP was 38 per cent for China, compared with the ratio of 16.4 and 15.5 for the US and Japan respectively. On the surface, China is even more 'open' than the US and Japan. So China could afford to be more internally oriented from now on.

This view cannot be pushed too far. China is such a large and diversified country that it should indeed make use of the economies of scale in some sectors and need not be overly dependent on international division of labour in other sectors. The fact that China is entering a new phase of infrastructure-led, heavy-industry-driven growth also means that domestic demand would play a more important role than in the 1980s. China should certainly not imitate the developmental experience of small open economies like Hong Kong and Singapore which, after all, did not face much choice.

However, several contrary considerations are noteworthy. First, China is not as open as it appears. The ratio of external trade to GNP, at 38 per cent in 1992, would be substantially revised downwards if the denominator, that is China's GNP, is evaluated on a PPP-adjusted estimation. As mentioned above, the IMF and World Bank estimates inflate it by four to six times. So a more 'accurate' ratio for China could be below ten per cent, so that the country is as yet much less 'open' than the US or Japan. Second, China's domestic market potential is still hampered by a number of factors: the low level of overall development (a per capita GNP of US$2,000-plus on a PPP-adjusted basis is still less than that of Sri Lanka or Peru),[45] widening income inequality and regional disparity (which has led to a polarization of purchasing power and consumption patterns), as well as the underdevelopment of transportation and communications networks, on the one hand, and urbanization on the other. 'Yuppies' in Shanghai and Shenzhen may be spending conspicuously like their counterparts in Manhattan or Tokyo, but several hundred miles away, in Anhui and Hunan, many people are still struggling with the basics of living.

All these shortcomings require time and resources to remedy. This brings us to the third point, that is China's need to absorb large amounts of foreign capital for its economic take-off. Without a huge injection of outside funds, China cannot quickly modernize its infrastructure, extend an efficient transportation network into its vast hinterland and help the rural areas urbanize and industrialize, and revamp and expand its secondary and tertiary sectors. What is involved is not just money but also technology and managerial expertise. In any case, if foreign capital is forthcoming, China

would have to service them by earning sufficient foreign exchange. So
exports still need to grow. Recently, in response to the Mexican financial
crisis, the Chinese government has shown increasing caution towards over-
exposure to foreign debts.[46] After all, a balance needs to be maintained in a
country's external fund flows. Overall, China will continue to raise its
degree of external orientation in trade and investment in the coming decade.
How to manage a progressively open China, which prides itself as a
'socialist market economy', is a task that undoubtedly requires courage,
vision and flexibility.

CONCLUSION

From a purely economic perspective, the trend seems to be well established
for both Hong Kong and Taiwan to be further integrated with the Chinese
economy through trade expansion and capital investment. Nevertheless,
while Hong Kong has already gone past the point of no return, Taiwan is
still trying to keep a distance. As analysed above, although cross-strait
investment and trade undoubtedly bring great benefits, the Taiwan
government is wary of the problems of over-dependence on China and the
'hollowing out' of its domestic industries. It has launched the 'Economic
Revitalization Programme' and has endorsed the setting up of the APROC
to broaden its economic base. Recently, it has also been promoting a policy
of 'southern expansion', which aims at extending its economic relations
with countries in South East Asia.

These moves may actually be economically beneficial as a diversified
Taiwan would be able to contribute more to the dynamism within Greater
China, although mainland China is expectedly worried about the political
implications, particularly concerning Taiwan's efforts to create a situation
of *de facto* independence. As far as trade is concerned, there is certainly a
case for upgrading the exports of Greater China as a whole, and there have
recently been proposals for setting up China–Taiwan science parks through
joint ventures in the mainland. As long as quick money can be earned easily,
such efforts would require farsightedness on the part of government as well
as entrepreneurs.

Greater China is no doubt one of the most dynamic growth areas in the
world. However, for each of the member economies, various kinds of
problems exist. While the integration process has generated strong growth
momentum, it has also produced some undesirable consequences which
need to be addressed. For other economies in the Asia Pacific region, the
case of Taiwan would probably be of more reference value than that of
Hong Kong, in so far as the negative impact of economic integration cum
political influence is concerned. Taiwan, given its historical development
pattern, larger size and more solid economic base, as well as the more
proactive policies of the authorities, is apparently in a better position to take
advantage of the economic integration with mainland China while reducing
the adverse side-effects, compared with freewheeling Hong Kong.

Problems within mainland China, the locomotive in the integrative economic entity that is emerging in the region, seem to be the most serious, particularly on the socio-political front. Nevertheless, this author's calculated guess is that it could muddle through the difficulties, and the doomsday scenario will not materialize.

Further development in intra-regional integration in the economic circle will continue to be heavily influenced by politics. Even an already captive Hong Kong will not be spared. The recent tension across the Taiwan Strait, which is linked to the deterioration in Sino–US relations, has apparently been a result of transitional politics as mainland China moves towards a post-Deng regime and as Taiwan shifts into a presidential-parliamentary system. It has been aggravated by Taiwan's bid to create more 'international space' for itself and the tide of the Taiwan independence movement. It also reflects the uncertainty in international geo-politics in the era after the Cold War.[47]

A military confrontation in the Taiwan Strait, particularly if it involved the United States, would derail the whole situation and throw open many possibilities. In any case, while such a scenario cannot logically be ruled out, a useful historical reference is the turbulence of 1989 in China and the subsequent downs and ups. Prophecies of imminent collapse, which flooded the global media in the aftermath of 1989, turned out to be largely moody projections of the day. For objective analysis, it is necessary to go beyond volatile politicking and look at the fundamentals. The 'Deng whirlwind' of 1992 created a dramatic shift in world opinion about the Chinese economy, which was excessive, just as the post-1989 predictions of disasters. All in all, the logic of economic interests may be powerful enough to convince everyone that even the more formidable political barriers could eventually be overcome.[48] Moreover, given the high degree of external orientation in the three constituent economies, Greater China looks likely to be increasingly open to the rest of the world, for both trade and capital flows. The fear of an awakening superpower, ready to bully Asia and the West, seems to have been overplayed. In per capita GNP/GDP terms, Greater China as a whole (not to mention mainland China alone) is unlikely to become the world's number one at least before the middle of the 21st Century.

ACKNOWLEDGMENTS

This paper is part of the findings of a research project on China's open policy funded by the Hong Kong Baptist University (FRG/93-94/I-01). The author wishes to thank the University as well as an anonymous referee of the Asia Pacific Business Review for useful comments.

NOTES

1. *Statistical Yearbook of China 1994*, pp.506 and 527.
2. For a discussion of the economic relations between China and the other Asian economies on the Pacific Rim, particularly the South East Asian ones, see John Wong, 'China in the Dynamic Asia Pacific Region', Keynote Speech in the Nineth Annual Conference of the Chinese Economists Society, Chicago, USA, 21 August 1994.

3.   'Taiwan Economic Statistics', *Industry of Free China*, Taiwan, various issues.
4.   *Estimates of GDP*; *Annual Digest of Hong Kong*; Hong Kong, various issues.
5.   Vincent C. Siew, 'Taiwan's Economic Development: the Present Situation and the Main Tasks to be Undertaken', Industry of Free China, Taiwan, Vol.83, No.2, March 1995, p.51.
6.   *Statistical Yearbook of China 1994*, p.21.
7.   See Tsang Shu-ki, 'So Far So Good for Chinese Economy', *Sunday Post*, Hong Kong, 7 August 1994.
8.   The World Bank, *World Development Report 1992*, Table 30.
9.   See Tsang Shu-ki, 'China the Third Largest Economy in the World?' *Ming Pao Daily*, Hong Kong, 16 June 1993, p.33.
10. The World Bank, *World Development Report 1993*, Table 30.
11. See Table 2 above.
12. See *Ta Kung Po*, Hong Kong, 14 September 1994.
13. *Hang Seng Economic Monthly*, Hong Kong, June 1993.
14. See Lin Wulong, 'The Development of Mainland China's Economy and Trade and the Relations between the Two Sides of the Strait: Review and Outlook', *Industry of Free China*, Taiwan, Vol. 83, No.2, pp.7–17.
15. For example, an economist in Taiwan estimated that on top of the indirect exports of US$4667.2 million to China through Hong Kong in 1991 (see Table 3), another amount of US$2880 million was 'transshipped' to the Mainland, making a total of US$7.55 billion of Taiwanese exports across the Strait. It represented 50.3% of Taiwan's exports to Hong Kong in the year. See Lin Yujun, 'Hong Kong's Contribution to Taiwan-Mainland Economic and Trade Exchanges', *Economic Outlook*, Chung-hua Institution for Economic Research, Taipei, Taiwan, No.29, January 1993.
16. For more detailed analysis of China–Taiwan trade, see Sun Yun-wing, *The China–Hong Kong Connection: the Key to China's Open Policy*, (Cambridge University Press, 1991); Sung Yun-wing, 'Illegal Trade between mainland China and Taiwan', paper presented at the International Pacific Rim Conference, Western Economic Association, 8–13 January 1994, Hong Kong; and Lin Yujun, 'Again on the Statistical Problems of Trade with the Mainland', *Economic Outlook*, Chung-hua Institution for Economic Research, Taipei, Taiwan, No.25, January 1992.
17. *South China Morning Post*, 'Business Post', 10 April 1995, p.1.
18. *United Daily*, Hong Kong, 13 April 1995, p.23.
19. See Table 3 and Lin Wulong, 'The Development of Mainland China's Economy and Trade', op.cit.
20. See Table 2.
21. Speech delivered at the 14th Meeting of Science and Technology Advisory Group (STAG), September 8, 1993, Taipei; reprinted in *Industry of Free China*, Vol. 80, No.4, October 1993.
22. See Tsang Shu-ki, 'Inflation', in Joseph Y.S. Cheng and Paul C.K. Kwong (eds), *The Other Hong Kong Report 1992* (The Chinese University Press, 1992), pp.425–45; and Tsang Shu-ki, 'Economic Integration between Hong Kong and Guangdong: Structural and Developmental Problems' (in Chinese), paper presented at the Conference *Guangdong-Hongkong Relations: Towards the Twenty-first Century*, organized by the Guangdong Academy of Social Sciences and the Economics Department of the Hong Kong Baptist University, Guangzhou, China, 9–10 December 1994.
23. For a more detailed discussion of the political economy of Hong Kong in the run-up to and beyond 1997, see Tsang Shu-ki, 'The Economy', in Donald H. McMillen and Man Si-wai (eds), *The Other Hong Kong Report 1994* (The Chinese University Press, 1994), pp.125–48.
24. See Sung Yun-wing, *The China–Hong Kong Connection*, op.cit.
25. See Tsang Shu-ki, 'Income Distribution', in Choi Po-king and Ho Lok-sang (eds), *The Other Hong Kong Report 1993* (The Chinese University Press, 1993), pp.361–68.
26. See Hu Len-kuo, 'Taiwan's Overall Development into the Next Century', paper presented at the International Conference on *Chinese Cities and China's Development*, organized jointly by the Centre of Urban Planning and Environmental Management and the University Graduates Association of the University of Hong Kong, 8–9 November 1993, Hong Kong.
27. *United Daily*, Hong Kong, 9 April 1995, p.11.
28. See Table 2 above.
29. Even at US$20 billion, Taiwan's stock of investments in China would equal only 10% of her GNP in 1993. In comparison, Hong Kong's GDP was US$115.1 billion in the same year, while her investments in China totalled US$103.9 billion (see Table 2). The ratio was therefore 90.3%, nine times that of Taiwan!

30. There are also economists who do not see any signs of 'hollowing out' in the Taiwan economy. See for example Lin Wulong, 'Analysis of the Problem of `Hollowing Out' in Taiwan', *Industry of Free China*, Vol.80, No.4, October 1993, pp.1–6.

31. See, for example, Gao Chang and Wang Zhicong, 'The Effects of Taiwan Investments in China on Cross-Strait Trade', paper presented in the Conference *Economic Development on Both Sides of the Strait and Asian-Pacific Economic Cooperation*, organized by the Chinese University of Hong Kong, Hong Kong, 9–10 June 1994.

32. Council for Economic Planning and Development, *The Six-year National Development Plan of the Republic of China*, January 1991.

33. See *Cross-Strait Economics and Trade*, Taiwan, No.37, January 1995, pp.5–6.

34. Chi Schive, 'Regional Operations Center and the ROC Economy in the 1990s', *Industry of Free China*, Vol.81, No.2, February 1994, pp.43–53.

35. The poll was conducted by a Taiwanese newspaper on 27 July 1995, right after the completion of the missile tests. See *China Times*, Taiwan, 28 July 1995. A poll in mid-July before the tests yielded a support rate of 18% for independence.

36. See Tsang Shu-ki, 'Current Problems in the Chinese Economy' (in Chinese), *Wide Angle*, Hong Kong, December 1992.

37. *Statistical Yearbook of China 1994*, Tables 16.2 and 16.3.

38. See Tsang Shu-ki, 'Current Problems in the Chinese Economy', *Wide Angle*, Hong Kong, December 1992.

39. See Wu Jinglian, 'Some Reflections on the Choice of Reform Strategy', *Jingji Yanjiu* (Economic Research), February 1987, pp.3–14.

40. See Christine P. Wong, 'Fiscal Reform and Local Industrialization: The Problematic Sequencing of Reform in Post-Mao China', *Modern China*, Vol.18, No.2, April 1992, pp.197–227; Tsang Shu-ki, 'Towards a System of Modernized Macroeconomic Control in China', paper presented at the 34th ICANAS (International Congress of Asian and North African Studies) Meeting, Hong Kong, August 1993; and Tsang Shu-ki and Cheng Yuk-shing, 'China's Tax Reforms of 1994: Breakthrough or Compromise?', *Asian Survey*, Vol.34, No.9, September 1994, pp.769–88.

41. Tsang Shu-ki, 'China Faces the Danger of the Loss of Control', *Wide Angle*, Hong Kong, July 1993.

42. See Tsang Shu-ki and Cheng Yuk-shing, 'China's Tax Reforms of 1994: Breakthrough or Compromise?', op. cit.; Tsang Shu-ki, 'Towards Full Convertibility? China's Foreign Exchange Reforms', *China Information*, Vol.9, No.1, Summer 1994, pp.1–41; and Tsang Shu-ki, 'Financial Restructuring', in Lo Chi-kin *et al.* (eds), *The China Review 1995*, (The Chinese University Press, Hong Kong), Ch.21.

43. The World Bank, *China Foreign Trade Reform: Meeting the Challenge of the 1990s*, A World Bank Country Report, 1994.

44. For such a possible trap in the case of China–Hong Kong economic links, see Tsang Shu-ki, 'Economic Link-up between Hong Kong and Guangdong: Structural and Developmental Problems', paper presented at the Conference *Guangdong-Hongkong Relations: Towards the Twenty-first Century*, organized by the Guangdong Academy of Social Sciences and the Economics Department of the Hong Kong Baptist University, Guangzhou, China, 9-10 December 1994.

45. See the World Bank, *World Development Report 1993*, Table 30.

46. See for example the report by *Asian Wall Street Journal*, 8-9 April 1995, p.1.

47. I have discussed about the possibility of a 'new Cold War' pitting China against the US, in which the latter might play the 'Taiwan card'. See Tsang Shu-ki, 'Hong Kong Caught in the Midst of a New Cold War?', *Ming Pao Daily*, Hong Kong, 2 December 1992. Such a 'new Cold War', if it really unfolded, would be very different in nature from the old one, as the integration of China into the world economy contrasts sharply with the isolation of the former Soviet Union.

48. Similar optimism about economics eventually prevailing over politics is shared by another commentary. See Merrill Lynch, 'Beijing-Taipei Relations', *The China Monthly*, 15 August 1995.

Foreign Direct Investment in China:
An Examination of the Literature

STEFAN KAISER, DAVID A. KIRBY and YING FAN

INTRODUCTION AND BACKGROUND

In 1978, after an era of political and economic isolation under Mao Zedong, China announced its 'open-door' policy, permitting foreign direct investment (FDI) into the country. Having experienced investment activities of foreign companies before the Communist Party came to power in 1949, China ended FDI in the early 1950s. State-owned joint companies with the Soviet Union were the only form of foreign investment which remained, those enterprises being also terminated in the late 1950s and turned over to the Chinese.[1] Thus, up to 1978, China's economy was largely closed off from the world economy. FDI was prohibited for historical, ideological and practical reasons.[2]

Since 1974, the Communist Party leaders have been directing China towards its long-term national goal, the modernization up to world standards of agriculture, industry, science, and national defence by the year 2000. At the *Third Plenary Session of the Eleventh Central Committee of the Communist Party* in December 1978, the new leadership, headed by Deng Xiaoping, restated that the primary national objective of China was to achieve these 'Four Modernizations'.[3] Chinese authorities also recognized that the only way to pursue this ambitious goal was to attract FDI which would provide the capital, the management skills and the technology that was lacking. Woodward and Liu[4] have estimated the technological gap between China and the developed countries to be between ten and 30 years. Thus, the absorption of FDI was seen as a vehicle to more sophisticated technology, and in the 1980s, China had been one of the largest importers of technology in the world.[5] Further, Chinese officials believed that partnerships with foreign companies could facilitate access to international markets which would absorb the country's exports and generate the foreign exchange needed to finance China's imports.[6] Finally, China has viewed foreign investment as a means of conserving funds for building and accelerating the pace of construction, learning about management and using the markets of foreign capital. Child[8] suggests that the new policy was both an immediate reaction to the shortcomings of the Cultural Revolution and a desire to exceed the limitations of the Soviet-style, centralized system developed in the first half of the 1950s. The new policy was based on a consensus that the economic failings of the Mao period had to be corrected.

Stefan Kaiser, David A. Kirby and Ying Fan, Durham University Business School

With the establishment of an institutional and legislative infrastructure, investment conditions were improved and became more attractive and secure. The promulgation in 1979 of the *'Law on Joint Ventures Using Chinese and Foreign Investment'* was the first step. The *'Regulations for the Implementation of the Law of the People's Republic of China on Joint Ventures Using Chinese and Foreign Investment'* followed in September 1983.[9] In October 1986, the State Council issued 22 *'Regulations Concerning Encouragement of Foreign Investment'* which offered foreign funded enterprises preferential treatment and operational freedom. A further step of improvement for investment conditions was an *'Amendment to the Law of the People's Republic of China on Joint Ventures Using Chinese and Foreign Investment'* in April 1990.

This 'open-door' policy has proved to be very successful. From 1979 to the end of 1994, more than 220,000 foreign funded ventures were approved, with contracted investment of US$300 billion and US$95 billion of utilized investment,[10] making the country the most important recipient of FDI in the developing world.[11] The 1994 figures show that the 'Middle Kingdom' absorbed roughly half the total for all developing countries.[12]

The aim of this paper is to analyse the phenomenon of FDI in China. It examines the different forms and composition of FDI, reviewing its development since the early days of the 'open-door' policy and analysing its importance to the Chinese domestic and export industries, as well as Western investor companies. Furthermore, the paper focuses on the world-wide sources of FDI in China and its distribution by both region and industry. Additionally, it reviews the existing research on FDI in China, emphasizing the investment mode of the equity joint venture (EJV). The article's objective is to provide both a 'hard', economic framework for FDI in China, and a 'soft' research framework, based on an examination of the literature. The article is divided into two main sections, the analysis of FDI in China (the 'hard' framework) and the analysis of the literature on joint ventures (JV) in China (the 'soft' framework).

FDI IN CHINA – AN ANALYSIS

The purpose of this section is to analyse inward FDI in China emphasizing the forms of FDI, its composition, its development since 1979, its importance for China's domestic and export industries and for foreign investors, the investment sources and its regional and industrial sector distribution.

The Forms of FDI in China

FDI, exporting and licensing are the three archetypal methods of servicing foreign markets. Ding[13] discovered four distinctive types of FDI in the People's Republic of China, namely the EJV, the contractual joint venture (CJV), the wholly foreign-owned enterprise (WOS) and the co-operative development. These four types of FDI were are also suggested by Wei[14] who examined the economic impact of the 'open-door' policy on China's growth. He argues that Chinese official statisticians also count compensation trade[15] as FDI. However, Kueh[16] suggests that this form has lessened in importance over time with its share in FDI declining from about 20 per cent in the early 1980s to less than five per cent in 1990. Analysis of the statistics for previous years suggests that the importance of compensation trade as a form of FDI has become negligible or is no longer counted as FDI, or both.

FIGURE 1
FOUR DISTINCTIVE TYPES OF FDI IN CHINA

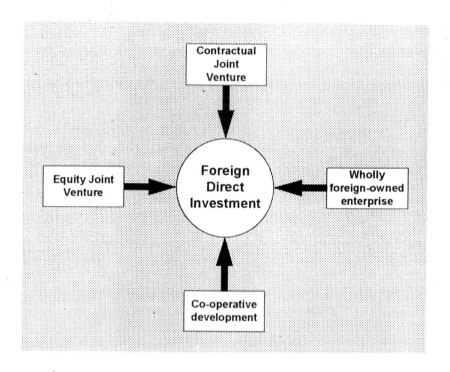

Equity joint venture: The EJV has a separate legal status and takes the form of the limited liability company formed in accordance with China's law on Chinese-foreign EJVs, first adopted by the *Second Session of the Fifth National People's Congress* in July 1979. Chinese and foreign partner(s)[17] contribute to the registered capital and take profits, risks and losses in proportion to that contribution. The *minimum* 25 per cent joint venture foreign-equity can be contributed in the form of cash, intellectual property, machinery and equipment or other tangible assets. The contribution of the Chinese partner is similar. In addition, the Chinese partner provides the right to use the site on which the JV is located. The EJV is usually managed jointly – under the direction of a board of directors, generally selected by the investors in proportion to their respective share of equity investment. Only after a revision of the EJV law in April 1990 was the board of directors of the joint venture allowed to be chaired by the foreign partner.

Contractual joint venture: The CJV subsumes a variety of arrangements whereby the Chinese and the foreign partner(s)[18] co-operate in joint projects and business activities according to the terms and conditions stipulated in a venture agreement. In contrast to the EJV, the CJV does not necessarily require the creation of a new legal entity. Authors[19] even rule out the formation of a new entity. The CJV can take any form of agreement and provides, therefore, more flexibility in negotiation than the EJV. However, CJVs share many characteristics with EJVs since, with most contracts, the partners contribute capital in a variety of forms (for example, cash, buildings, equipment and know-how) towards a project that runs for a specified duration.[20] Pearson[21] adds that the partners often negotiate rights and obligations and manage the ventures jointly.

Wholly foreign-owned enterprise: The WFOE is a venture without any contribution from a Chinese partner. It is financed and managed solely by the foreign investor. Since WFOEs were not perceived by the Chinese as transferring significant amounts of technology or management skills to China, the development of this form of FDI has been somewhat limited. Thus, the WFOE is offered fewer investment incentives by the Chinese government and faces more stringent requirements on balancing foreign exchange earnings and expenditures. Until April 1986, the government refused to approve WFOEs.[22] Only as China's experience with FDI has increased has the country become more open to the approval of such ventures. Since 1988, when the Chinese government began making a special effort to attract WFOEs, they have become more important. The fear of technology leakage through licensing agreements or JVs may be one of the reasons why WFOEs are experiencing increasing popularity amongst foreign investors. WFOEs are typically manufacturing plants which their owners have established for reasons of land availability and cheaper labour.[23]

Co-operative development: Co-operative development is mainly employed in the exploration and development of offshore oil resources. It has only a small share of all FDI in China.

Composition of FDI in China

The EJV is the most common form of FDI in China.[24] It is the form most preferred by both the foreign and the Chinese partner,[25] since JVs are not only a channel for inward investment into China but provide the means for the import of technological knowledge and managerial skills.[26] Almost two out of three foreign-funded enterprises are JVs.[27] It has been particularly favoured by foreign investors due to its ability to obtain assistance from the authorities. Until April 1986 as mentioned above the Chinese government refused to approve wholly foreign-owned enterprises,[28] making JVs virtually the only vehicle for FDI. However, while the JV was the most preferred form of investment in the first decade since the opening up of the Chinese economy, the WFOE is now developing. Various studies[29] have shown that after the promulgation in 1986 of the law governing WFOEs, the number of wholly foreign-owned ventures increased from 18 in 1986 to 2,795 in 1991, though China's *Ministry of Foreign Economic Relations and Trade (MOFERT),*[30] suggests there were 6,081 WFOEs at the end of 1991.

Of the 220,000 or more foreign funded projects, approved by the end of 1994, 63.3 per cent were EJVs, 15.6 per cent were CJVs and 21.1 per cent were WFOEs.[31] A comparison of these percentage figures with the composition of FDI in China by the end of 1991[32] reveals that the investment mode of the EJV became more important, increasing its share from 54 to 63.3 per cent. Overall, the importance of the EJV as a form of FDI in China has increased. Table 1 presents the accumulated frequency of the individual forms of FDI in China during the period 1979–94.

TABLE 1
ACCUMULATED FREQUENCY OF THE INDIVIDUAL FORMS OF FDI IN CHINA
DURING THE PERIOD 1979–94

Number of Firms

Form of FDI in China	No.*	(%)
Equity joint venture	139,260	63.3
Contractual joint venture	34,320	15.6
Wholly foreign-owned enterprise	46,420	21.1
TOTAL FDI	220,000	100

Note: Since the total number of FDI projects by the end of 1994 exceeds 220,000, the individual data represent rather underestimated figures
Source: Ministry of Foreign Trade and Economic Cooperation, MOFTEC (Beijing), August 1995.

Development of FDI since 1979

Table 2 reviews the development of FDI in China from the formation of the first JV, *Beijing Air Catering*, in 1980,[33] to more than 220,000 foreign-funded ventures, with a total contractual investment of US$300 billion, and a utilized investment of US$95 billion approved by the end of 1994.[34] As the table reveals, there has been a steady flow of FDI to China. However, 1986 witnessed a dramatic slow-down in the rate of growth of FDI inflow. Glaister and Wang[35] suggest that this was caused by problems affecting China's economy and the effect of those problems on JVs, whilst Chua and Kin-Man[36] consider JV management problems as responsible for the decrease in relative growth. However, the slow-down of foreign investment in 1986 appears to have been caused by the introduction of austerity measures in 1985, following a gross overheating of the economy in the mid-1980s, when a severe balance of payments problem emerged.[37]

TABLE 2
DEVELOPMENT OF FDI IN CHINA 1979–94

Investment

Year	Projects No.	Contracted (US$, bn)	Utilized (US$, bn)
1979–82	922	6.01	1.17
1983	470	1.73	0.64
1984	1,856	2.65	1.26
1985	3,073	5.93	1.66
1986	1,498	2.83	1.87
1987	2,233	3.71	2.31
1988	5,945	5.30	3.19
1989	5,779	5.60	3.39
1990	7,273	6.60	3.49
1991	12,978	11.98	4.37
1992	48,764	58.12	11.0
Subtotal	*90,791*	*110.46*	*34.35*
1993	83,000	111	21.3
1994	46,209	78.54	39.35
TOTAL	220,000	300	95

Note: Due to the fact that the total FDI by the end of 1994 accounts for more than 220,000 projects, the derived figures for 1994 might be affected by minor inaccuracies.
Source: Data series 1979–92: Statistical Yearbook of China 1993, State Statistical Bureau, Beijing, in Child *Management in China During the Age of Reform*, Cambridge 1994, p.216. Data 1993 (projects and pledged investment): *Financial Times*, 15 June 1994. Data 1993 (utilized investment): *Financial Times*, 4 November 1995. Data 1979–94 (total): *International Business*, 8 June 1995. Data 1994 derived from the other series.

Analysing Table 2 reveals a first big jump in foreign direct investment activities in China in 1992 when foreign companies established more projects (116 per cent), worth more of pledged investment (111 per cent) than in the complete period 1979–91. However, utilized investment in 1992 reached only 47 per cent of the investment utilized in the preceding 13 years. In 1993, China experienced an even steeper rise. Some 83,000 new projects were approved, 70 per cent more than the year before. This new contribution of foreign-funded projects nearly equalled (91.42 per cent) the total of projects approved in the previous 14 years. The projects approved in 1993 accounted for some US$111 billion worth of contractual and US$21.3 billion worth of utilized investment which is an increase over the previous year of 91 per cent and 94 per cent respectively. In 1994, the foreign investment activities of foreign enterprises slowed significantly – at least with respect to the number of projects and the value of contractual

investment. In 1994, Chinese authorities approved only 46,209 new
projects, worth some US$78.54bn of contractual investment, which
accounts for 71 per cent of the contracted investment in 1993. Some 56 per
cent of these were approved the year before, however. In terms of utilized
investment only, 1994 experienced a steep increase with US$39.35 billion
or 85 per cent more than in 1993. Table 3 presents the results of the growth
analysis of foreign direct investment to China in the years 1979 to 1994.

TABLE 3
GROWTH ANALYSIS OF FDI TO CHINA

Year	Projects	Investment	
	No.	Contracted (US$, bn)	Utilized (US$, bn)
1979–91	42,027	52.34	23.35
1992	48,764	58.12	11.0
1992 of 1979–91 period	116.03%	111.04%	47.11%
1979–1992	90,791	110.46	34.35
1993	83,000	111	21.3
1993 of 1979–92 period	91.42%	100.49%	62.01%
1993 of 1992	170.21%	190.98%	193.64%
1979–1993	173,791	221.46	55.65
1993 of 1979–93 period	47.76%	50.12%	38.27%
1994	46,209	78.54	39.35
1994 of 1979–93 period	26.59%	35.46%	70.71%
1994 of 1993	55.67%	70.76%	184.74%
1979–94	220,000	300	95
1994 of 1979–94 period	21.00%	26.18%	41.42%

Noteworthy, however, is the fact that the figures for FDI in China are
frequently inconsistent. For instance, Daniels et al.[38] suggest a total of 89
JVs being established with partners from 14 different countries by the fall
of 1983. This figure must be treated with considerable caution, as it would
suggest an increase of only six JVs over the previous year. This seems
unlikely. Further, the US$25.8 billion of utilized investment for the year
1993, as suggested by the *Economist*[39] of 30 April 1994, was confirmed by
the *Financial Times*[40] of 15 June 1994 proposing US$26 billion but it was
adjusted down to US$21.3 billion by the *Financial Times*[41] only a few
months later. Again, Child[42] suggests that the years 1992 and 1993 saw a
veritable explosion of FDI to China with US$169 billion of newly
contracted and 167,500 foreign-funded ventures by the end of 1993.
However, figures on the basis of the 1979–92 data from the *Statistical
Yearbook of China 1993* and figures from the *Financial Times* suggest the
total number of projects by the end of 1993 to be 173,791.

Importance of FDI for China's Economy

FDI is of considerable importance to China's domestic and export industries. Foreign-funded production of technical and consumer goods, as well as the provision of services, has reinforced the output power of the Chinese economy. Foreign-funded enterprises account for more than eight per cent of the industrial output and fixed asset investment[43] in an economy which, for the past decade, has been growing at anything between four and 14 per cent per year.[44] Other sources[45] extend these findings, stating that in the period 1978–93 the economy expanded at a compound annual rate of nine per cent a year with an overall increase of 260 per cent. This was the longest period of high and relatively stable expansion since 1949.[46] However, between 1978 and 1992 the proportion of the industrial output contributed by state-owned companies dropped from 80 per cent to 48 per cent[47] and by 1994, GDP was growing at only 11.8 per cent,[48] as a result of the Central government's attempt to 'cool down' the economy and thus stem inflation.

Foreign-financed production contributed approximately one third of the economy's foreign exchange income in 1994, after 25 per cent by mid-1993.[49] China's merchandise exports grew from US$53 billion in 1989 to US$91 billion in 1993, making the country one of the ten largest trading nations in the world by the end of 1994.[50] From 1978 to 1990, China's average annual rate of trade expansion was some 15 per cent and its share of the world trade almost doubled during this period.[51] Since its 'opening up', the country's exports have expanded at an average annual rate of 16 per cent, enabling China to improve its export position from 32nd in 1978 to 13th in 1989. In 1993, the year when the People's Republic achieved a trade surplus with America of US$23 billion,[52] foreign-funded firms accounted for 27.5 per cent of China's exports and for all of the growth in its exports over 1992.[53] In the first six months of 1994, the export activity of foreign-funded enterprises increased by approximately 45 per cent over the same period in 1993, and by the end of 1994, exports exceeded imports by US$5.3 billion[54] compared with a deficit of US$12.2 billion in 1993.[55] For 1995, experts predicted a trade surplus of US$7 billion.[56]

Wei,[57] in his article examining the contribution of exports and FDI to China's rapid industrial growth, states that there is 'clear evidence that during the period 1980–90 more exports are positively associated with higher growth rates across Chinese cities', while Glaister and Wang[58] discovered that most of the large and mid-size JVs are aimed at the domestic market, whereas the smaller manufacturing JVs are export oriented. Wei[59] further argues that the superb growth rates of the coastal areas relative to the national average (9.2 per cent from 1988 to 1990) can be explained entirely by their effective use of exports and FDI. In addition to the direct effects of FDI on the Chinese economy, such as the infusion of capital, Wei[60] suggests that the contribution of FDI comes in the form of technological or managerial know-how to those firms that interact with foreign invested/managed firms through various channels, as well as to those that receive foreign investment direct or under foreign management.

Importance of FDI for Foreign Investors

The importance of FDI for foreign firms is at least twofold. First, investors in China are pursuing strategic considerations as part of their global strategy. The Chinese market provides a large potential for investing enterprises in terms of size and, increasingly, quality. Thus, entry into the Chinese market is important for foreign enterprises.[61] De Bruijn and Jia[62] also argue that entry to the Chinese market is an important strategy for many multinational companies (MNCs) from the US, Japan and Western Europe. Western MNCs fear that Japanese competitors could attain leadership in the Chinese market which could result in cost reductions, helping to undercut prices in the US or third country markets. This was considered by Daniels *et al.*[63] as a reason for Western investors seeking a strategic presence in China. A part of the German car manufacturer Volkswagen's global strategy, for instance, is to establish a business base in the Far East to limit the dominance of Japanese firms.[64] Second, it has been suggested by Newman[65] that foreign firms migrate to China as their positions in home markets decline.

Sources of FDI into China

Since the early days of China's 'open-door' policy, the immense flow of investment capital into the country has been dominated by ethnic Chinese investors from Hong Kong and Taiwan.[66] Hong Kong has been the major investor both in terms of the number of projects and capital invested, and at the end of 1992 it accounted for some 60 per cent of all FDI to China.[67] Between 1984 and 1990, Hong Kong's share of FDI was above 50 per cent for every single year except 1985, when it was 48.9 per cent.[68] Beamish and Wang[69] found that up to 1984, more than three quarters of all JV investment in China came from Hong Kong and Macao, the Portugese colony, whereas the US, Japan and Europe accounted for only seven, 6.6 and 3.7 per cent, respectively. It should be noted, however, that a proportion of the Hong Kong investment is Taiwanese capital disguised for political reasons and another proportion is mainland China capital disguised to take advantage of the preferential treatment of foreign investment in China. This is termed *round trip investment.*[70] As Kueh[71] suggests, however, the bulk of the Hong Kong investment is genuine Hong Kong capital.

More recent figures of the ten largest investing countries, covering the period 1979–94, are presented in Table 4. These figures do not indicate a remarkable change in the above ranking. Hong Kong/Macao still leads the list, followed by Taiwan, the US, Japan, Singapore and European investor countries, such as the UK and Germany. South Korea is likely to figure highly as a venue for FDI. Since the establishment of diplomatic relations with China in 1992, South Korea's investment has been growing. In the first half of 1993, for instance, the Chinese government approved 274 South Korean projects worth some US$327 million after approving 286 projects (US$239 million) in the whole of 1992.[72] While South Korea was not on the list of the top ten investors in 1993, the country ranked seventh, ahead of Thailand and Germany, in 1994.

TABLE 4
FDI IN CHINA IN THE PERIOD 1979–94. THE TOP TEN INVESTORS

Rank Country Projects	Contracted Investment	
	(No.)	(US$, bn)
1 Hong Kong/Macao	139,959	200.39
2 Taiwan	27,002	23.61
3 United States	16,257	20.73
4 Japan	10,322	14.23
5 Singapore	4,567	8.63
6 UK	1,017	5.8
7 South Korea	4,247	3.78
8 Thailand	1,967	2.9
9 Germany	892	2.72
10 Canada	2,178	2.7

Source: Foreign Investment Administration, MOFTEC (Beijing), 12 June 1995.

Regional Distribution of FDI in China

China's coastal areas were the first regions targeted for the country's economic development. Up to 1992, they absorbed more than 80 per cent of the total capital.[73] This confirms findings by Glaister and Wang[74] who suggest that 76 per cent of the JVs they surveyed were located in the coastal areas. However, the inflow of FDI has taken place in three distinctive investment areas.

Area one is China's five Special Economic Zones (SEZs), Shenzhen, Zhuhai and Shantou in *Guangdong Province*, Xiamen in *Fujian Province* and *Hainan Province,* all of them on the Southeast coast. The first four SEZs were created in early 1979. Encouraged by the rapid development in these SEZs, the central government in 1983 declared the entire island of Hainan in the South China Sea as a 'special area open to foreign investment'. In 1988, Hainan was declared a 'Super SEZ' and was given provincial status with greater authority to attract foreign business.[75] With those SEZs, China provided administrative entities which allowed the application of a more liberal set of investment incentives to attract foreign business ventures. In the SEZs, foreign investors could expect preferential treatment with respect to tax incentives, flexible arrangements for land use with reductions in charges, reduced welfare contributions, flexible arrangements for employing labour and the possibility of preferential prices for raw materials and equipment.[76] Ruggles[77] suggests that China has considerably improved the infrastructure in the SEZs. However, the unique role of SEZs as attractions for foreign investment declined after the first phase of the investment policy.[78]

Area two is the so-called 'Open Areas' along China's East and Southeast coast. In the spring of 1984, the Chinese government designated 14 major coastal cities[79] as 'open cities' and granted them many of the privileges it had earlier reserved for SEZs. These 'Open Cities' were given greater autonomy in economic policy making, were allowed to offer special incentives (such as tax holidays) to encourage FDI, and were authorized to set up special districts, so-called 'Economic and Technological Development Zones' in which they created a particularly favourable economic environment for foreign investors. A range of 'Open Economic Zones' was created during the second half of the 1980s - some by the central government in Beijing, some by provincial and local authorities. These were allowed to offer a variety of privileges and special treatment for foreign investors. Three of these were established in September 1985.[80] Child[81] suggests that the incentives and special provisions available to foreign investors in economic zones are normally similar to those available in the 14 coastal cities. In 1992, these 'Open Areas' received some 82.3 per cent of all contracted inward investment. Phillips[82] suggests that the 'open cities' offered better possibilities than the SEZs since, in most cases, the existing infrastructure, industrial bases, managerial and technical personnel and numbers of skilled workers were superior than in the SEZs.

Area three consists of the remaining inland provinces. They are backward in terms of both their economy and their infrastructure. Compared with these inland areas, the more developed central, mainly coastal, cities such as Shanghai, Tianjin, and Beijing have been the most favoured recipients of EJVs.[83] However, as the mainly preferred central and coastal areas are gradually becoming too expensive for many investors, FDI will eventually spread to these vast inland provinces. This is in line with the intention of the Chinese government. According to Fan,[84] while FDI to areas such as Guangdong, Hainan and Beijing declined dramatically in 1992, the proportion of investment to China's hinterland increased by 60.9 per cent to an overall contracted inward investment share of 17.7 per cent.

Due to their proximity, Guangdong and Fujian are the most favoured investment locations for investors from Hong Kong and Taiwan, respectively, whereas China's Northeast was primarily targeted by Japanese and Korean investors.[85]

Distribution of FDI to China by industry

Woodward and Liu[86] argue that most of the JVs established in China are engaged in the exploitation of natural fuels, labour-intensive manufacturing or tourism and infrastructure-projects, such as highways, railways and port development.

Since the beginning of the 1980s, Hong Kong and Japanese firms have invested in the textile, pharmaceutical, food, motorcycle, and electronics industries. In addition, enterprises from America and Europe have invested capital in the automotive, chemical, machinery and coal industries.[87] Fan[88] suggests that manufacturing, as well as real estate and services, are the industries which have received the most foreign investment. In 1992, the proportion of manufacturing dropped slightly, whereas real estate and services increased by 40 per cent. A potential reason for this might be China's priority for new investment to improve its poor infrastructure. Latest available figures[89] reveal that 74.1 per cent of the total foreign capital by the end of 1994 was invested in the industry sector, 14.3 per cent in the real estate and services sector, 2.5 per cent in agriculture and less than ten per cent in infrastructure projects. This is summarized in Table 5. The proportion of telecommunications and power generating industries is set to increase in the 1990s, as the Asia Pacific region is likely to spend more on telephones and power than any other region in the world.[90]

TABLE 5
DISTRIBUTION OF FDI BY INDUSTRY SECTOR

Sector	Projects	
	No.*	(%)
Industry	163,020	74.1
Real Estate and Services	31,460	14.3
Agriculture	5,500	2.5
Infrastructure	20,020	9.1
TOTAL	220,000	100

* Since the total number of FDI projects by the end of 1994 exceeds 220,000, the individual data represent rather underestimated figures.
Source: Ministry of Foreign Trade and Economic Cooperation, MOFTEC (Beijing), August 1995.

Data Problems

Figures on FDI in China provided by different sources show a great variance in accuracy. This can lead to serious difficulties if Chinese data are to be compared either with those of other countries, or over time.[91] In order to avoid erroneous assumptions and conclusions, statistics on FDI in China must be treated with care since:

• There is no strong tradition of reporting economic statistics in China.[92]
• The collection and reporting of statistical data describing the pattern of investment is fragmented, with the resultant data not always being consistent.[93]
• Both the definition and calculation of FDI in China vary from source to source. For instance, equity from the Chinese side is often included in the total value of projects or JVs in some cases, which exaggerates the size of the actual inflow of foreign capital.
• It has not yet been clarified how much of the invested capital is 'round-trip' investment, that is, investment which has been invested in foreign enterprises by Chinese companies and is now being re-imported to China by the foreign company in order to make use of the preferential treatment of FDI.[94]

•   A natural time lag exists between the signing of a contract and the actual operation of the business. Woodward and Liu[95] suggest as a possible reason for this delay the complex bureaucratic procedures which have to be followed when investments are set in motion. In a considerable number of cases, foreign-funded enterprises received the contracted investment only after being in operation for two years or more. In addition, many foreign businesspeople, after agreeing to invest, take time to assess the investment climate and production conditions before placing their investment. Recently, China started checking *how much* capital investors are actually bringing into the country. In one case, equipment provided by the foreign partner in a printing JV was found to have a true value of only US$ 500,000, though it was supposedly worth more than US$2.6 million.[96]

•   Western publications do not always report data on FDI in China consistently, as the following example shows: The *Financial Times* of 31 August 1994[97] discussed the sources of FDI into China, ranking the US (with pledged investment worth some US$78.47 billion) number two amongst the ten largest investor countries by the end of 1993 after Hong Kong (US$150.9 billion), but ahead of Taiwan (US$18.4 billion) and Japan (US$8.9 billion). France was considered the fifth largest investor (US$6.84 billion). In its issue of 7 November 1994, the same publication[98] considered the US (now with investments of US$14.6 billion) as having been overtaken by Taiwan (now having invested some US$18.46 billion), and France was not even listed in the list of the top ten investors.

EXISTING RESEARCH

It is commonly held that doing business in China has attracted great interest amongst the academic community.[99] In particular, JVs are currently receiving increasing attention.[100] After building the 'hard' framework of FDI in China, the second part of this article establishes the 'soft' framework, examining the existing body of research as identified in the published literature. It reveals that studies may be classified according to:

•   Level of the study
•   Stage in the JV life cycle
•   Perspective of the foreign partner
•   Size of the participating foreign partner

Level of the study: The knowledge of the level at which a study is based allows the identification of the organizational point of view of the author. *Micro-level* studies usually adopt an internal company perspective, drawing conclusions from case studies or sample surveys, and trying to explain certain behavioural aspects of the firm based on political, economic or sociocultural variables. *Macro level* studies on the other hand examine the political, economic or sociocultural environment in the first instance, and then try to derive some suggestions for individual cases, if any at all.

Stage in the JV life cycle: Particularly interesting for the examination of the literature is the identification of the individual stage of the JV life cycle. For the purpose of this examination, two major stages in the JV life cycle are distinguished:

• Preparation and creation phase: This deals with issues such as partner selection, negotiation, investment motivation, perceptions and objectives for engaging in a joint venture.
• Implementation, operation and management phase: This covers issues such as performance of the JV in relation to ownership and control, sharing JV management and management style.

Perspective of the foreign partner: Another dimension of interest is the origin of the foreign partner and particularly whether, and to what extent, the strong presence in terms of investors from Hong Kong, Taiwan, USA, Japan and Europe is reflected in the key literature.

Size of the participating foreign partner: Business publications such as the *Financial Times* frequently report on the establishment of JVs in China between local Chinese partners and companies from America and Western Europe. In most of the cases, however, the Western partner is an MNC, whereas information on the joint venturing of small and medium sized businesses (SMEs) is rare. Thus, this review of the literature also examines whether, and to what extent, the JV experiences of SMEs are examined.

Methodology

A three-directional methodological approach has been applied in order to identify the key contributions on Sino-foreign JVs in periodicals about China published in the period 1980–94. Yang[101] identified key sources of information on doing business with China. He discussed periodicals published in the US, UK, Hong Kong and China, all published in English. However, only a few of these publications provide an editorial environment for *qualitative* studies on Sino-foreign JVs in China. A second source of literature on Sino-foreign JVs were databases such as ANBAR and ABI. Keyword searches led to a variety of potential contributions. However, only a small number of academic articles met the selection requirements outlined above. Finally, bibliographies of already reviewed contributions in the area of interest were analysed and papers of potential value selected.

Findings

The search and selection process resulted in a sample of 32 papers approaching the phenomenon of the Sino-foreign JV in China. All of them were in English and covered the period between 1980 to 1994.

Level of the study: As Table 6 reveals, the majority of studies (68.75 per cent) in the sample approached the Sino-foreign JV topic at the micro level.

Fewer (18.75 per cent) are at the macro level.[102] The remaining studies (12.50 per cent) are micro/macro level investigations. Studies by Nehemkis and Nehemkis,[103] Wu,[104] Phillips[105] and Ruggles[106] have examined the legal-regulatory and political environment, while other authors[107] have studied the cultural environment. All these publications recognize the need to adjust thinking and business practices to the Chinese environment, which is different from the environment Western investors are used to. The studies suggest that only enterprises which practise a form of political, legal and cultural understanding will succeed in doing business with, and in, China. However, relatively few studies discussed the legal-regulatory environment. This contradicts the earlier findings of Daniels *et al.*[108] and Wei.[109] These authors argue that most of the studies carried out so far focus on the legal-regulatory and political environment of JVs in China. The findings of the study might lead to the conclusion that in recent years writers have discussed, increasingly, problems located *in* the JV rather than the problems surrounding it. After 15 years of 'open-door' policy in China, it might be expected that investing companies will have gained experience in preparing and operating JVs and have identified the short- and long-term problems which need to be researched.

TABLE 6
LEVEL OF STUDY

Level of Study	Studies	
	No.	(%)
Micro	22	68.75
Macro	6	18.75
Micro/Macro	4	12.50
TOTAL	32	100

Stage in the JV life cycle: Table 7 reveals that the majority of the studies examined have undertaken investigations into the preparation and creation of JVs as the first phase in the JV life cycle. The study found that the motivations for entering into a JV and the negotiating of a JV have attracted a major share of the attention of writers.[110] The studies also present descriptions of the experiences of firms in China.[111] Some studies in the sample[112] carried out research into the transfer of technology. Finally, most papers[113] provide some guidelines for negotiating, successfully, JVs with potential Chinese partners. However, only a few[114] deal with the actual problems of managing joint businesses between Western and Chinese partners. This confirms the earlier findings of Baird et al.[115]

TABLE 7
STAGE IN THE JV LIFE CYCLE

Stage	Studies No.
Preparation/Creation	13
Implementation/ Operation/Management	5

Nationality of the foreign partner: As Table 8 reveals, in at least 49 per cent of all the cases investors from the US were investigated. Several studies did not provide detailed specifications of their samples. It may be assumed that these non-specified cases are based on analyses of US enterprises, since their authors are American. However, more studies than expected[116] researched European investment in China. With regard to the recency of these studies this paper argues that the increasing commitment of European firms in China appears to be reflected to an increasing extent in the literature. In addition, Glaister and Wang[117] suggest that UK firms are increasingly looking to China as a feasible location for overseas investment.

TABLE 8
NATIONALITY OF FOREIGN PARTNER

Foreign Partner	Studies No.	(%)
US	21	48.84
Europe	10	23.26
Australia/ New Zealand	2	4.65
Japan	2	4.65
Hong Kong	2	4.65
Several	2	4.65
No specification	4	9.30
TOTAL	43[*]	100

* The total number of 43 is a result of double entries if a study discussed more than one case.

Size of the participating foreign partner: Most of the papers investigate FDI in China by large MNCs. This is shown in Table 9. Very few[118] recognize the need to research, also, the investment experiences of SMEs. The majority of the studies do not specify, explicitly, the size of the foreign investor in the JV investigated. However, it would be false to assume that these papers examine SMEs only.

TABLE 9
SIZE OF FOREIGN PARTNER

Size of Foreign Partner	Studies No.	(%)
MNC	11	34.38
SME	1	3.12
MNC and SME	1	3.12
No specification	19	59.38
TOTAL	32	100

SUMMARY

For a decade and a half, FDI in China has been increasingly popular. It is seen by the Chinese as a vehicle to realize the ambitious goal of the *'Four Modernizations'*. Up to 1978, China had no experience with FDI in Western terms. Some authors[119] argue that the country was not entirely unfamiliar with FDI having had joint companies with the Soviet Union. Child[120] suggests that many of the larger, capital-intensive state enterprises were developed with Soviet assistance during the 1950s (and thus tended to be concentrated in the North of China). However, this paper does not support the point of view that these partnerships can be understood as forms of FDI, since these business relationships were on the state level, rather than the company level and since the Chinese and the Soviets shared a similar ideology. It becomes evident, however, when analysing Child's above finding that 'the Soviet Union developed state enterprises'.[121] Zamet and Bovarnick[122] agree, suggesting that China has had very little experience in the past with Western business practices. China's 'open-door' strategy has been very successful. The EJV is the most common and popular form of FDI in the country and the number of FDI contracts has been increasing steadily since 1980. In 1986, FDI inflow to China slowed dramatically. More than 220,000 foreign funded ventures had been approved by the end of 1994.

FDI is important for China's domestic and export industries. Ethnic investors from Hong Kong and Taiwan have dominated FDI to China. Within the European Union, the UK is still the largest investor. However, Germany is catching up. The coastal areas are the most preferred regions for FDI but increasingly the hinterland is attracting foreign investment. Telecommunications and power generating industries, and their financing needs, are set to increase within the next decade. However, figures on FDI in China are often inaccurate and have, therefore, to be treated with caution. The literature on JVs reveals that the majority of studies have been carried out on the micro rather than a macro level, contradicting earlier findings. A reason for this might be the increasing interest in the internal problems of JVs. The paper also found that the majority of studies investigated the preparation and creation stage of JVs in China. The actual management problems are widely neglected.[123] Further, the study found that most of the investors surveyed are of American origin and that investigations into the investment of SMEs are the exception.

CONCLUSION

The existing amount of FDI in China is far from sufficient in relation to the capital China needs to modernize its economy. A recent estimate by a leading Chinese economist put the figure required for the rest of the decade at around US$1,000 billion.[124] From 1979 to 1991, FDI contributed only 43.4 per cent of the total amount of capital inflow to China. Foreign governments and international financial institutions provided the lion's share. In 1993, portfolio investment had reached 24 per cent of FDI.[125] After an immense inflow of direct investment to China in 1993, the country registered a slow downturn in 1994 as a result of inflation, overheating and other factors on the mainland.[126]

Western investors still face structural, organizational and legal problems for their investments. China's failure to respond, adequately, on intellectual property rights and trade disputes serves as recent evidence for this. Although Chinese officials have repeatedly assured the West that the country's FDI policy will be long-term, the attitudes of Western investors are still affected by uncertainty about China's future political direction after the death of Deng Xiaoping.

Encouraged by their governments, European companies are increasingly engaging in FDI in China. They provide a great potential for research. This study suggests that American companies sill represent the majority of cases discussed. Even periodicals such as the *Management International Review*, a German publication, widely ignore German or European investment in China. Further, when investigating JVs in China, authors frequently survey cross-industrial samples, implicitly assuming that their findings are not affected by the fact that respondents stem from different industries which, for instance, might receive different treatment by the Chinese government. Thus, it is proposed that future studies should carry out either single-industry research or comparative cross-industry research, rather than the non sector-specific studies which have characterized the investigations to date.

The study also reveals that most research has been carried out on MNCs and it appears to be assumed that the findings from large MNCs are also applicable to SMEs. Tsang,[127] for instance, provides evidence to disprove this assumption. Thus, there is a need for research into the experiences and management problems of SMEs as they attempt to penetrate the Chinese market through the establishment of JVs. Finally, on the evidence provided here, further research is required into the management of JVs in China. Little is known about the problems that occur when managing cross-cultural, cross-national joint businesses. Issues such as the management of personnel, finance and marketing in Sino–foreign JVs need to be addressed more frequently than appears to have been the case to date.

NOTES

1. F.W. Wu, 'The Political Risk of Foreign Direct Investment in China: A Preliminary Assessment', *Management International Review*, Vol.22 (1982), pp.13–25. Wu suggested that the Sino–Soviet relations were terminated in 1955, whereas Child argues that the Sino–Soviet relations split in 1960. J. Child, *Management in China During the Age of Reform* (Cambridge, 1994).

2. D.Z. Ding, 'Control Strategy and Performance of US–Chinese Joint Ventures' (Unpublished PhD thesis, University of California, Los Angeles, 1993).

3. The *Four Modernizations* were first announced in 1975.

4. D.G. Woodward and B.C.F. Liu, 'Investing in China: Guidelines for Success', *Long Range*

Planning, Vol.26 (1993), pp.83–9.

5.   E.W.K. Tsang, 'Strategies for Transferring Technology to China', *Long Range Planning*, Vol.27 (1994), pp.98–107.

6.   Child, Management in China.

7.   L. Yuanzheng, 'The Chinese Economy and Foreign Experience: A Chinese Economist's View', *Australian Journal of Chinese Affairs*, Vol. 3 (1980), pp.70.

8.   Child, Management in China.

9.   R. Ruggles, 'The Environment for American Business Ventures in the People's Republic of China', *Columbia Journal of World Business*, Vol.18 (1983), pp.67–73. A good overview of the development of the legislative environment of FDI in China is provided by K.W. Glaister and Y. Wang, 'UK Joint Ventures in China: Motivation and Partner Selection', *Marketing Intelligence and Planning*, Vol.11 (1993), pp.1–15.

10.   Wendepunkt der chinesischen Investitionspolitik, *International Business*, 8 June 1995, p.23.

11.   Big, *The Economist*, 30 April 1994, p.97.

12.   Quick, quick, slow, *The Economist*, Survey China, 18 March 1995, pp.6–12. Earlier the *Financial Times* (T. Walker, 'Projects grow in size', *Financial Times Survey CHINA*, 7 November 1994, p.VI.) presents exactly 50 per cent and in its issue of 5 December 1994 (T.Walker, 'China investment flows surge', *Financial Times*, 5 December 1994, p.4) the publication presents 33 per cent as the share of FDI to developing countries being absorbed by China.

13.   Ding, thesis.

14.   S.J. Wei, 'Open Door Policy and China's Rapid Growth: Evidence from City-Level Data', *National Bureau of Economic Research*, Working Paper No. 4602, December (1993).

15.   Through compensation trade, foreign firms provide machines or product designs to Chinese enterprises and obtain a part of the output as payment.

16.   Y.Y. Kueh, 'Foreign Investment and Economic Change in China', *China Quarterly*, 131, September (1992), pp.637–90.

17.   The joint venture has to have at least *one* Chinese and *one* foreign partner.

18.   As n.17.

19.   Such as Child, Management in China.

20.   Ibid.

21.   M.M. Pearson, *Joint Ventures in the People's Republic of China: The Control of Foreign Direct Investment under Socialism* (Princeton, 1991).

22.   B. Gomes-Casseres, 'Joint Ventures in the Face of Global Competition', *Sloan Management Review*, Vol.30 (1989), pp.17–26.

23.   Child, Management in China.

24.   Woodward, 'Investing in China', pp.83–9.

25.   Ding, thesis.

26.   Child, Management in China.

27.   Y. Fan, 'Foreign Direct Investment in China: A view from the inside', Working paper (Durham University Business School, 1994).

28.   Gomes-Casseres, 'Joint Ventures in the Face', pp.17–26.

29.   Tsang, 'Strategies for Transferring Technology', pp.98–107. Ding, thesis.

30.   MOFERT was formed in March 1982 to encourage and supervise foreign economic relations. It was succeeded by MOFTEC in 1993.

31.   According to the Ministry of Foreign Trade and Economic Cooperation (MOFTEC) in Beijing, August 1995.

32.   see Ding, thesis.

33.   O. Shenkar, 'International Joint Ventures' Problems in China: Risk and Remedies', *Long Range Planning*, Vol.23 (1990), pp.82–90.

34.   Wendepunkt der chinesischen Investitionspolitik, *International Business*, 8 June 1995, p.23.

35.   Glaister, 'UK Joint Ventures in China', pp.1–15.

36.   B.L. Chua and G.T. Kin-Man, 'Managing Joint Ventures in China: A Cross-Cultural Approach to Motivation and Quality', *International Journal of Management*, Vol.10 (1993), pp.294–99.

37.   Find details on the foreign exchange difficulties of several large domestically-oriented JVs in R. Pomfret, 'Ten Years of Direct Investment in China', *Asian Perspective*, Fall/Winter (1989).

38.   J. Daniels, J. Krug, and D. Nigh, 'US Joint Ventures in China: Motivation and Management

of Political Risk', *California Management Review*, Vol.27 (1985), pp.46–58.

39. Big, *The Economist*, 30 April 1994, p.97.
40. T. Walker, 'Foreign investment in China slows', *Financial Times*, 15 June 1994, p.3.
41. M. Wolf and T. Walker, 'A continent discovered', *Financial Times*, 4 November 1994, p.15.
42. Child, Management in China.
43. Thoburn et al, investigating Hong Kong enterprises' direct investment in China, suggest that China has received much genuine transfer of technology from labour-intensive, export-oriented, activities. J.T. Thoburn, H.M. Leung, E. Chau and S.H. Tang, *Foreign Investment in China Under the Open Policy – The Experience of Hong Kong Companies*, (Aldershot and Brookfield: 1990).
44. Competing for capital, *The Economist Asian Finance Survey*, 12 November 1994, p.34.
45. M. Wolf, 'Baffling questions for China-watchers', *Financial Times Survey CHINA*, 7 November 1994, p.IV. Wei ('Open Door Policy and China's Rapid Growth') suggests that the average annual growth rate of China's GDP from 1980 to 1990 was 9.5 per cent.
46. Child, Management in China.
47. Ibid.
48. China seeks to restrict growth to 9 %, *Financial Times*, 11 January 1995, p.3.
49. Beijing Review 1993, p.28.
50. Gattsmacked, *The Economist*, Survey China, 18 March 1995, pp.17–19.
51. Wei, 'Open Door Policy and China's Rapid Growth'.
52. Reaching an impasse, *The Economist*, 6 August 1994, p.56.
53. Gattsmacked, *The Economist*, Survey China, 18 March 1995, pp.17–19.
54. Kaiser, S. 'Deutsch-chinesischer Handel und deutsche Investitionen in China – Ein Update', *CHINA-INFO*, No. 19 (1995), Newsletter published by Delegation of German Industry and Commerce Shanghai.
55. T. Walker, 'Reform momentum slows down', *Financial Times Survey CHINA*, 7 November 1994, p.I.
56. Kaiser, S. 'Deutsch-chinesischer Handel und deutsche Investitionen in China – Ein Update'.
57. Wei, 'Open Door Policy and China's Rapid Growth', p.3.
58. Glaister, 'UK Joint Ventures in China', pp.1–15.
59. Wei, 'Open Door Policy and China's Rapid Growth'.
60. Ibid.
61. M.E. Porter, *Competitive Strategy* (New York, 1980).
62. E.J. de Bruijn and X. Jia, 'Transferring Technology to China by Means of Joint Ventures', *Research–Technology Management*, January–February (1993), pp.17–22.
63. Daniels, 'US Joint Ventures in China', pp.46–58.
64. E.J. de Bruijn and X. Jia, 'Managing Sino–Western Joint Ventures: Product Selection Strategy', *Management International Review*, Vol.33 (1993), pp.335–60.
65. W.H. Newman, 'Launching a Viable Joint Venture', *California Management Review*, Vol.35 (1992), pp.68–80.
66. Tsang, 'Strategies for Transferring Technology', pp.98–107. Daniels, 'US Joint Ventures in China', pp.46–58.
67. Fan, 'Foreign Direct Investment in China'.
68. Wei, 'Open Door Policy and China's Rapid Growth'.
69. P.W. Beamish and Y. Wang, 'Investing in China via Joint Ventures', *Management International Review*, Vol.29 (1989), pp.57–64.
70. Wei, 'Open Door Policy and China's Rapid Growth'.
71. Kueh, 'Foreign Investment and Economic Change in China'.
72. 'China and Korea: Moving towards industrial cooperation – Interview with Korea's Embassador', *Chinese Entrepreneur*, October 1993.
73. 'An analysis of FDI utilized in China since 1979', *China Industrial Economics Research*, No.10, 1993.
74. Glaister, 'UK Joint Ventures in China', pp.1–15.
75. Ibid.
76. Child, Management in China.
77. Ruggles, 'The Environment for American Business Ventures', pp.67–73.
78. Glaister, 'UK Joint Ventures in China', pp.1–15.
79. These cities were: Beihai, Dalian, Fuzhou, Guangzhou, Lianyungang, Nantong, Ningbo, Qingdao, Qinhuangdao, Shanghai, Tianjin, Yantai, Wenzhou, Zhanjiang.

80. Glaister, 'UK Joint Ventures in China', pp.1–15.
81. Child, Management in China.
82. C.H. Phillips, 'China in Transition', *Columbia Journal of World Business*, 20th Anniversary Issue (1985), pp.53–6.
83. Glaister, 'UK Joint Ventures in China', pp.1–15.
84. Fan, 'Foreign Direct Investment in China'.
85. Ibid.
86. Woodward, 'Investing in China', pp.83–9.
87. de Bruijn, 'Transferring Technology to China', pp.17–22.
88. Fan, 'Foreign Direct Investment in China'.
89. According to Ministry of Foreign Trade and Economic Cooperation, Beijing, August 1995.
90. Hype and glory, *The Economist Asian Finance Survey*, 12 November 1994, p.27.
91. M. Wolf, 'Baffling questions for China-watchers', *Financial Times Survey CHINA*, 7 November 1994, p.IV.
92. R. Pomfret, *Investing in China: Ten Years of the 'Open Door' Policy* (Harvester Wheatsheaf, 1991).
93. Shenkar, 'International Joint Ventures' Problems', pp.82–90.
94. Pomfret, *Investing in China*.
95. Woodward, 'Investing in China', pp.83–9.
96. A trickle or a flood?, *The Economist*, 6 August 1994, p.65.
97. T. Walker, 'US companies sign up for $5bn of new business in China', *Financial Times*, 31 August 1994, p.4.
98. Walker, 'Projects grow in size'.
99. L.P. Yang, 'Business in China – Current Information Sources', *Asia Pacific Journal of Management*, Vol.7 (1990), pp.137–45. Tsang, 'Strategies for Transferring Technology', pp.98–107.
100. I.S. Baird, M.A. Lyles, and R. Wharton, 'Attitudinal Differences Between American and Chinese Managers Regarding Joint Venture Management', *Management International Review*, Special Issue (1990), pp.53–68.
101. Yang, 'Business in China', pp.137–45.
102. A sample of studies with macro perspective can be found in W.C. Wedley (ed.) *Changes in the Iron Rice Bowl: The Reformation of Chinese Management*, (London, 1992). The sample includes contributions on the effects, origins and tensions of China's managerial reform, Confucian influences in Chinese management, reformation of organizational behaviour, marketing practices and financial management.
103. P. Nehemkis and A. Nehemkis, 'China's Law on Joint Ventures', *California Management Review*, Vol.22 (1980), pp.37–46.
104. Wu, 'The Political Risk', pp.13–25.
105. Phillips, 'China in Transition', pp.53–6.
106. Ruggles, 'The Environment for American Business Ventures', pp.67–73.
107. I.H.S. Chow, A. Inn, and L.B. Szalay, 'Empirical Study of the Subjective Meanings of Culture Between American and Chinese', *Asia Pacific Journal of Management*, Vol.4 (1987), pp.144–151. B. Wilpert and S.Y. Scharpf, 'Intercultural Management – Joint Ventures in the People's Republic of China', *International Journal of Psychology*, Vol.25 (1990), pp.643–50. J.M. Zamet and M.E. Bovarnick, 'Employee Relations for Multinational Companies in China', *Columbia Journal of World Business*, Vol.21 (1986), pp.13–9.
108. Daniels, 'US Joint Ventures in China', pp.46–58.
109. Y. Wei, 'A Test for the 'Entry Mode Choice' in the Joint Ventures of the People's Republic of China', *International Journal of Management*, Vol.10 (1993), pp.288–93.
110. A.K.M. Au and P. Enderwick, 'Small Firms in International Joint Ventures in China: The New Zealand Experience', *Journal of Small Business Management*, Vol.32 (1994), 88–94. Daniels, 'US Joint Ventures in China', pp.46–58. W.H. Davidson, 'Creating and Managing Joint Ventures in China', *California Management Review*, Vol.29 (1987), pp.77–93. D.K. Eiteman, 'American Executives' Perceptions of Negotiating Joint Ventures with the People's Republic of China: Lessons Learned', *Columbia Journal of World Business*, Vol.25 (1990), pp.59–67. J. Frankenstein, 'Trends in Chinese Business Practice: Changes in the Beijing Wind', *California Management Review*, Vol. 29 (1986), pp.148–60. Glaister, 'UK Joint Ventures in China', pp.1–15. Newman, 'Launching a Viable Joint Venture', pp.68–80. Shenkar, 'International Joint Ventures' Problems', pp.82–90. S. Stewart and C.F. Keown, 'Talking with the Dragon: Negotiating in the People's Republic of China',

Columbia Journal of World Business, Vol.24 (1989), pp.68–72. C.L. Wagner, 'Influences On Sino–Western Joint Venture Negotiations', *Asia Pacific Journal of Management*, Vol.7 (1990), pp.79–100.

111. Daniels, 'US Joint Ventures in China', pp.46–58; Wei, 'A Test for the 'Entry Mode Choice'', pp.288–93.
112. de Bruijn, 'Transferring Technology to China', pp.17–22. S.R. Hendryx, 'Implementation of a Technology Transfer Venture in the People's Republic of China: A Management Perspective', *Columbia Journal of World Business*, Vol.21 (1986), pp.57–66. Tsang, 'Strategies for Transferring Technology', pp.98–107.
113. Newman, 'Launching a Viable Joint Venture', pp.68–80. Stewart, 'Talking with the Dragon', pp.68–72. Eiteman, 'American Executives' Perceptions', pp.59–67. Beamish, 'Investing in China via Joint Ventures', pp.57–64. P. Aiello, 'Building a Joint Venture in China: The Case of Chrysler and the Beijing Jeep Corporation', *Journal of General Management*, Vol.17 (1991), pp.47–64. L.S.T. Tai, 'Doing Business in the People's Republic of China: Some Keys to Success', *Management International Review*, Vol.28 (1988), pp.5–9.
114. Baird, 'Attitudinal Differences', pp.53–68. J. Child and L. Markoczy, 'Host-Country Managerial Behaviour and Learning in Chinese and Hungarian Joint Ventures', *Journal of Management Studies*, Vol.30 (1993), pp.611–31. Chua, 'Managing Joint Ventures in China', pp.294–99. J. Ireland, 'Finding the Right Management Approach', *The China Business Review*, January–February (1991), pp.14–7. R.L. Tung, 'Corporate Executives and Their Families in China: The Need for Cross-Cultural Understanding in Business', *Columbia Journal of World Business*, Vol.21 (1986), pp.21–5. See also Child, Management in China During the Age of Reform.
115. Baird, 'Attitudinal Differences', pp.53–68.
116. Stewart, 'Talking with the Dragon', pp.68–72. Tsang, 'Strategies for Transferring Technology', pp.98–107. Wilpert, 'Intercultural Management', pp.643–50. de Bruijn, 'Managing Sino–Western Joint Ventures', pp.335–60. Chua, 'Managing Joint Ventures in China', pp.294–9. Child, 'Host-Country Managerial Behaviour', pp.611–31. Glaister, 'UK Joint Ventures in China', pp.1–15. Ireland 'Finding the Right Management Approach', pp.14–7.
117. Glaister, 'UK Joint Ventures in China', pp.1–15.
118. Tsang, 'Strategies for Transferring Technology', pp.98–107. Au, 'Small Firms in International Joint Ventures in China', pp.88–94.
119. Woodward, 'Investing in China', pp.83–9. Wu, 'The Political Risk', pp.13–25.
120. Child, Management in China.
121. Ibid, p.16.
122. Zamet, 'Employee Relations for Multinational Companies', pp.13–9.
123. A detailed examination of Hong Kong companies' investments in China can be found in Thoburn, Foreign Investment in China under the Open Door Policy.
124. A positive analysis of the structure of foreign investment in China and policy suggestions. *Research on Economics and Management*, No.4, 1993.
125. The next revolution, *The Economist Asian Finance Survey*, 12 November 1994, p.4.
126. Lands of Opportunity, *Far Eastern Economic Review*, UK in Asia – A special advertising supplement, pp.44–8. Apart from the high rate of foreign capital inflow, two other factors cause China's inflation: the hugh capital demands of state-owned firms and the governments budget deficit.
127. Tsang, 'Strategies for Transferring Technology', pp.98–107.

Inequality, Inflation, and their Impact on China's Investment Environment in the 1990s and beyond

ZHAO XIAOBIN SIMON and
TONG S.P. CHRISTOPHER

INTRODUCTION

Spatial disparity or regional inequality of economic development in China has always been a topic of interest in contemporary China studies. Much has already been written about the inter- and intra-provincial, regional, and urban–rural inequalities in mainland China's recent economic reform and development.[1] Among them, most serious time-series studies can be seen in Lyon (1991) and Zhao (1996),[2] while the most recent studies of household income distributions can be seen in Khan *et al.* (1992) and Chai (1992).[3] However, these research projects, particularly those concerning spatial aspects, seem to lack two considerations. First, the prospect or projection of inequality in future, say in the later 1990s and beyond, has been largely neglected, although most research has shown some concern about the worsening of inequality in future.[4] Much of the effort and attention has been placed on what happened in the past, such as in Lyon (1991) and Zhao (1994a; 1996). Yet, what will happen in the next five or ten years or so appears a much more relevant and pressing question to address.[5] Second, the impact of inflation on spatial aspects has also been largely neglected. So far it has been very difficult, if not impossible, to find a piece of scholarly work that links inflation with spatial inequality. This does not refer to a study that uses an inflation deflator or 'real' (not nominal) data, but a research effort that focuses on spatialities or spatial impacts of inflation, which, as found in this article, have surprising features and implications for equality and distribution. Thus, this article intends to contribute to these two aspects within a more practical framework, and with spectial reference to investment and the business environment in China.

Inequality, including spatial disparity, and inflation have become increasingly explosive problems in contemporary China. In conjunction with an analysis of spatialities (spatial patterns) of inflation, this article examines the current trend of China's spatial disparities, in terms of economic output, real consumption, and real income, and in the realms of inter-provinces, inter-regions, and urban–rural divides. This article also focuses on the exploration of impacts of inflation on spatial disparities, and

Zhao Xiabin Simon and Tong S.P. Christopher, Hong Kong Baptist University on the combined effect of inflation and spatial disparity on China's investment and business environment in the 1990s. The findings of this article suggest that spatial inequalities in economic development and income distribution, especially since 1990, have been accelerated or exacerbated by high inflation, which appears to hit poorer areas disproportionately. Given the reinforcement of disparity and inflation and the current upsurges of rampant localism, the investment and business environment of China in the 1990s, in terms of political and social unrest and economic profitability, will be severely undermined and, therefore, increasingly uncertain. It is likely that this trend will extend beyond the turn of the century.

DATA AND METHODOLOGY

Among contemporary China studies it seems fashionable to criticize the fidelity of China's official data, notably data from China's Statistical Yearbook or Zhongguo Tonji Nianjan (ZGTJNJ), compiled by the State Statestical Bureau (SSB). This is particularly true of the figures for economic 'growth', 'income', and 'urban population'.[6] An analysis by Khan et al. (1992) reveals some striking differences between their own survey results and SSB's regarding China's rural and urban household income. For example, the figures for per capita rural income and disposable urban household income appear about 39 per cent and 55 per cent higher respectively, than the SSB figures, according to Khan et al.'s survey (in 1988).[7] The major differences come from the subsidies to housing, including rental value of owner-occupied housing, and other public subsidies and income in kind, all of which are excluded from the SSB's data.[8] Khan et al.'s analysis generally reveals the fact that both household income and inequality of the income distribution are underestimated in the SSB data.[9] However, although problems remain, the quality of work from the ZGTJNJ has substantially and steadily improved in the past 15 years and particularly since 1990. For example, tremendous effort has been channeled into including income in kind and subsidies in the disposable household income.[10] Currently, the ZGTJNJ is widely accepted and used to compile the principal indicators of equalities and living standards in China.[11]

Despite these drawbacks, data used in this paper is primarily from ZGTJNJ. Apart from the above general reasons, there are also three specific rationales supporting the use of ZGTJNJ in this research. First, in terms of personal/household income, SSB's data covers the major part of income. According to Khan et al.'s survey,[12] net cash income from productive activities (farming) in rural areas and wage income in urban areas are the largest sources of income for both groups. These two income categories, which have the most equalizing effects on distribution of income,[13] are sufficiently covered by the SSB's data. Second, the most serious weakness in the SSB's data is its lack of coverage of housing subsides and the rental value of owner-occupied houses, both of which also have very unbalancing effects.[14] However, higher housing subsidies do not necessarily mean higher income and living standards. Rather, it in fact means the opposite, lower living standard, as the subsidy is necessary only because of a shortage of housing. This situation usually occurs in large cities and in the eastern region, where inhabitants receive higher housing subsidies but enjoy less living space or a lower quality of living in terms of housing.[15] Thus, using data which includes housing subsidies in the caculation of spatial disparity (regional inequality) may have an unnecessarily misleading effect. Third, this paper focuses on a 'trend' analysis in a time-series or sequence. This 'trend' analysis not only requires the SSB's data,[16] but also can overcome its weaknesses, such as inaccuracy, lack of coverage, and reliability, since the analysis looks at trends over the entire researched period, rather than results from one individual year.

The main purpose of studying spatial disparity is to understand how the well-being of people differs from one area to another in a time-sequence. Therefore, three indicators have been chosen that are closely related to people's living standards. These indicators are GDP per capita, real private

FIGURE 1
CV OF PER CAPITA GDP (PROVINCES – REGIONS)

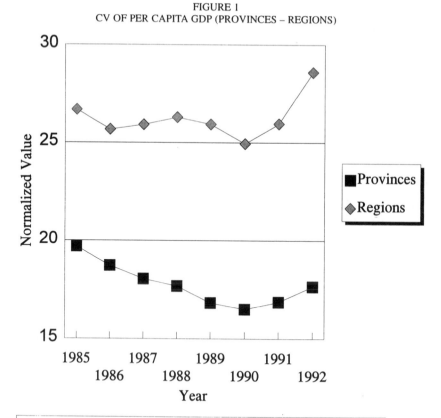

The units on Y-axis are normalized values.
The S.D of the two series are 0.027 and 0.014, respectively.

consumption per capita, and real income per capita.[17] For urban households, the deflated year-end urban household per capita cash income is used as their real per capita income. For rural households, the deflated year-end peasant household per capita net income is used as their real per capita income. All indicators are expressed in real terms, so all nominal variables have been deflated by using the inflation rate of the corresponding year. The inflation rate was calculated by using the retail price index. The data for all variables was collected from ZGTJNJ.[18] As an extension of the work of Lyons (1991) and Zhao (1996),[19] this study, with more enriched data input and a comprehensive framework, covers the period 1985–92.[20]

Spatial disparity will be investigated at three different levels: province, region, and urban–rural division. In exploring the degree of difference at the provincial level, data from 30 provinces, including Beijing, Tienjing and Shanghai and excluding Taiwan, were used. When analyzing the variation between regions, the whole nation has been divided into the eastern region, the central region, and the western region. There are a total of twelve provinces included in the eastern region, and nine included in each of the other two regions.[21]

To measure disparity, two well-established and most often used measures of dispersion have been selected, namely the coefficient of variation (CV)[22] and the standardized difference (See Appendix).

SPATIAL DISPARITIES OF ECONOMIC OUTPUT AND INCOME DISTRIBUTION

Per Capita GDP and Real Consumption Per Capita

The dispersion of per capita GDP and real consumption per capita will first be examined. Figure 1 shows the CVs of per capita GDP for both 30 provinces and three regions.[23] Before 1990, the trend for the series was generally falling. However, since 1990, the trend has turned into a rising one for both CVs, with the one of the regions rising at a faster rate. Therefore, the narrowing of inter-regional disparity as described by Lyons (1991)[24] is only true for the period before 1990. By 1992, the degree of inter-provincial disparity had almost returned to its 1987 level, and the degree of inter-regional disparity had in fact gone beyond its 1987 level. Therefore, one can conclude that, since 1990, the gaps of inter-provincial and inter-regional inequality have begun to widen.

Figure 2A shows the average values of real consumption per capita for the 30 provinces and three regions. It is clear that the average real consumption per capita for both provinces and regions has been rising continuously since 1985. However, although the average values have increased, Figure 2B reveals that, if we look at the corresponding CVs of the series, the dispersion of real consumption per capita has increased as well. From the value of 0.307 in 1985, the CV of 30 provinces has increased to 0.374 by 1991. For the three regions, the CV had increased from 0.142 to 0.204 in the same period.

FIGURE 2A
AVERAGE REAL CONSUMPTION PER CAPITA (PROVINCES – REGIONS)

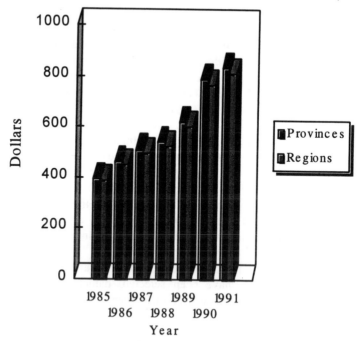

FIGURE 2B
CV OF REAL CONSUMPTION PER CAPITA (PROVINCES – REGIONS)

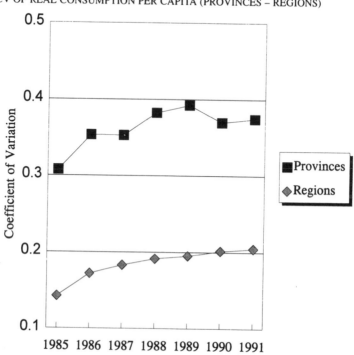

FIGURE 3A
URBAN-RURAL CONSUMPTION DIFFERENTIAL – AVG
(PROVINCES)

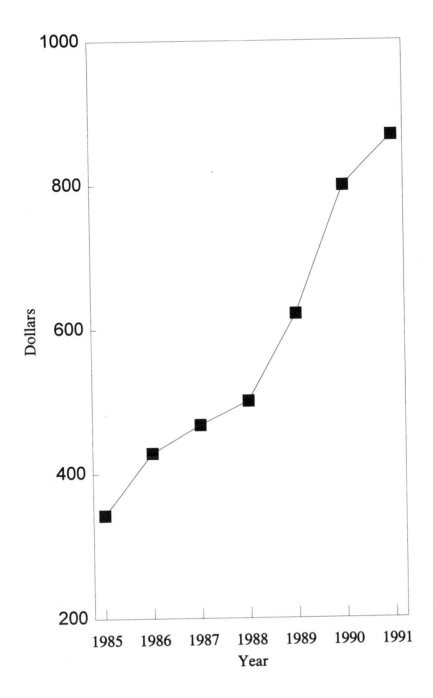

FIGURE 3B
URBAN-RURAL CONSUMPTION DIFFERENTIAL – CV
(PROVINCES)

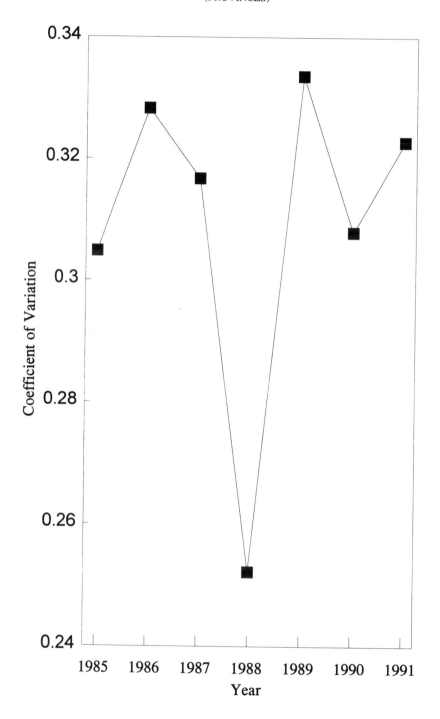

FIGURE 3C
URBAN-RURAL HOUSEHOLD CONSUMPTION DIFFERENTIAL
(NATIONAL)

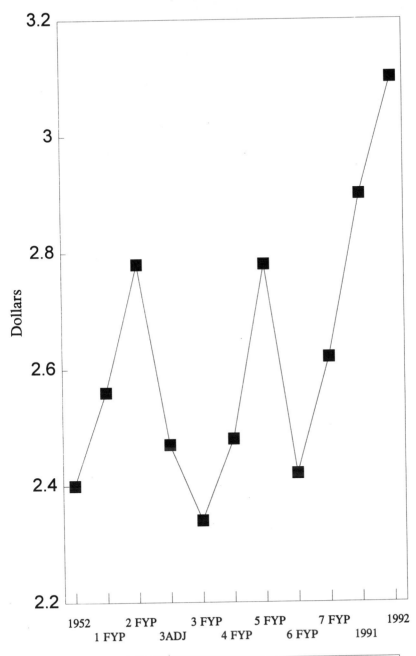

3ADJ stands for the three years adjustment period.
1FYP=1st Five Years Plan, 2FYP=2nd Five Years Plan, and etc.

The average urban and rural differential in real consumption per capita of the 30 provinces is shown in Figure 3A. The average of consumption differentials between urban and rural areas has also been continuously rising since 1985. Between 1985 and 1991, the real per capita consumption differential increased by 524.97 yuan. This result is another reflection of increased spatial inequality. In Figure 3B, the CV of consumption differentials between urban and rural areas for the 30 provinces demonstrates, not a simple rising or falling trend, but one depicted that is oscillating. Therefore, the differences in urban and rural consumption across the 30 provinces seem to be fluctuating from year to year. This conclusion is supported by trends in the average urban and rural household consumption differentials as calculated by the SSB (Figure 3C).[25]

Under the new political and economical environment, our findings show that both inter-provincial and inter-regional disparities in per capita GDP had decreased in the 1980s, but they have begun to increase since 1990, reversing a general down-turn trend. Although the average real consumption per capita has increased, its inequality of distribution has also increased as well. Lastly, the consumption gap between urban and rural areas has also been continuously rising since 1985.

Real Income Per Capita

To continue exploring spatial disparity, it is necessary to look at the dispersion of real income per capita, which is another indicator of well-being. Figure 4A incidcates the average value, CV, and standardized difference of real income per capita for the 30 provinces. While the average real income per capita has increased from 711.63 yuan in 1985 to 1678.58 yuan in 1992, its disparity of dispersion had increased as well. Within the same period, the CV and standardized difference rose by 0.08 and 0.48, respectively. Therefore, although urban reforms have successfully raised the average real income per capita, they have, on the other hand, also made the poor poorer and the rich richer. Figure 4B demonstrates the average value and the CV of real income per capita for the three chosen regions. The pattern of the series is similar to that in Figure 4A. Therefore, no matter whether at the provincial or regional level, one could come to the same conclusion that spatial disparity, in terms of real income per capita, has increased since 1985.

Besides examining differences among the provinces and the regions, it is also crucial to look at the inequality between urban and rural areas. In Figure 5A, the average income differentials between urban and rural areas for the 30 provinces and its corresponding CV is indicated.[26] Note that while the average income differential has increased from 654.14 in 1985 to 1703.54 in 1992, its CV, on the other hand, fell from 0.31 to 0.18 in the same period. These figures imply that people living in rural areas are earning less and less real average income per capita than people living in urban areas. Furthermore, the income gap between urban and rural areas is also becoming more and more alike from one province to another. As a second

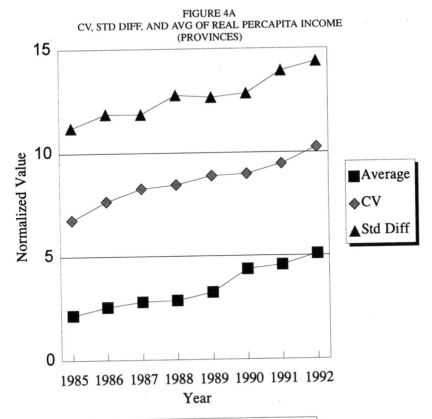

FIGURE 4A
CV, STD DIFF, AND AVG OF REAL PERCAPITA INCOME
(PROVINCES)

The units on Y-axis are normalized values. The S.D.
for three series are 330.34, 0.02, and 0.15, respectively.

reference, the household income differential between urban and rural areas
can be calculated by employing SSB data (Figure 5B).[27] The trend of the
series since 1985 is almost the same as the one presented in Figure 5A.
According to Khan *et al.*'s analysis, the SSB's figure is a more than ten per
cent underestimate of the true urban–rural difference, and China is an
extraordinarily high income differential country by the standards of other
developing countries in Asia (China's ratio is 2.19 in 1988 and 2.33 in
1992), even higher than Bangladesh (1.85 in the 1980s) and Indonesia (1.66
in 1987).[28]

In conclusion, in terms of real income per capita, when used as an
indicator of well-being, spatial disparity has increased at both the provincial
and regional level, just as the gap of income differential between urban and
rural areas has been enlarged since 1985. What is more, due to the
difference in the urban and rural income gap across provinces being
continuously narrowed, the unpleasant conditions experienced by people
living in different rural areas of the country are also seemingly alike.

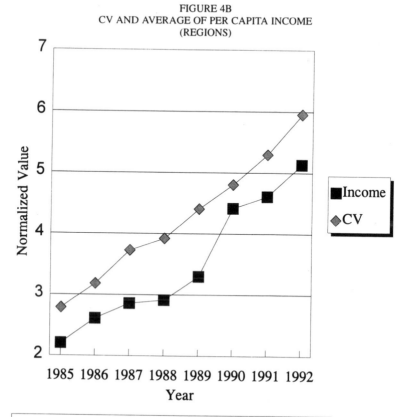

FIGURE 4B
CV AND AVERAGE OF PER CAPITA INCOME
(REGIONS)

The units on Y-axis are normalized values. The S.D.
for two sereis are 321.30 and 0.02, respectively.

INFLATION AND ITS SPATIALITIES

Since 1985, inflation in China has increased rapidly. Except for a short
period of economic retrenchment in 1990–91, the average inflation rate
between 1985 and 1993 has been mostly in double digits. Even under the
tight regulation of the government, following the experience of 1988–89,
inflation has recently re-emerged and reached an all-time high of 25 per cent
in October 1994. If we look at Figure 6, showing the average inflation rate
of the 30 provinces, and its corresponding CV whilst average inflation has
soared from 2.02 per cent to 23.08 per cent between 1990 and 1994, its CV
has dropped drastically from 0.98 to 0.15 within the same period. These
figures point to the fact that inflation has become a *national* phenomenon in
China. That is, inflation is no longer a problem of only the coastal or the
more economically developed provinces. From the decline of the CV, one
can infer that inflation exists also in less developed provinces.

Across the average inflation rates of all three regions, the eastern region
has the highest inflation rate during the first five years of 1985–89, but this

FIGURE 5A
URBAN-RURAL PERCAPITA INCOME DIFFERENTIAL
(PROVINCE)

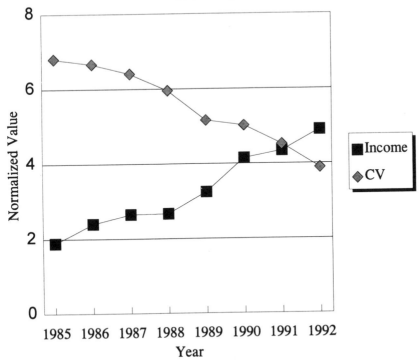

The units on Y-axis are normalized values. The S.D.
For two sereis are 347.81 and 0.05, respectively.

was not so in the last five years of 1990–94 (Figure 7A). In fact, when inflation reached its all-time high in October 1994, it was the central region that experienced the highest average inflation rate of 25.23 per cent. These results confirm our argument that inflation in China has become a national phenomenon. Figure 7B shows the CV of inflation rates for the three regions. Note that, when inflation was high in 1988–89 and in 1994, at between 18.10 and 23.08 per cent, its CV was relatively low, between 0.04 and 0.06. However, when inflation was low, particularly in 1990 when it reached 2.02 per cent, its CV was relatively high at 0.32. These numbers suggest that when average inflation was low, all three regions did not enjoy the same low price level. Yet, when average inflation was high, all three regions suffered the same high price level.

Information shows the average inflation rate differential between urban and rural areas serves to clarify two important points (Figure 8). Firstly, the difference between urban and rural average inflation rates has never been very large. The biggest difference between the two inflation rates is still within 4 per cent for the whole period. Secondly, it is not true that urban

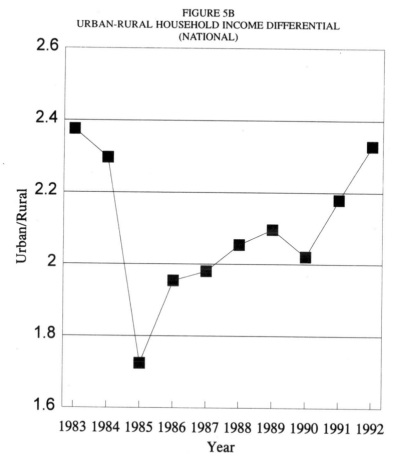

FIGURE 5B
URBAN-RURAL HOUSEHOLD INCOME DIFFERENTIAL
(NATIONAL)

areas always have a higher average inflation rate. In the years when the average inflation rate was high, the figure shows that it was the rural areas that experienced a relatively higher rate of inflation: 19.25 per cent for rural versus 16.82 per cent for urban areas in 1989, and 24.06 per cent for rural versus 22.2 per cent for urban areas in August of 1994. Even in 1990, when average inflation was low, rates were 3.06 and 1.14 per cent for rural and urban areas, respectively.

It is apparent that inflation in China has recently emerged as a national problem. Although, at the beginning of the urban reforms, inflation was always highest in the eastern region, it was the central or the western region that had the highest rate of inflation in the four of the five years between 1990 and 1994. Furthermore, the average inflation rate was higher in rural than in urban areas in 1989, 1990, and 1994. This spatial pattern of inflation suggests that inflation is a 'foot-loose' and mobile evil that hits the poor and rural areas disproportionally harder.

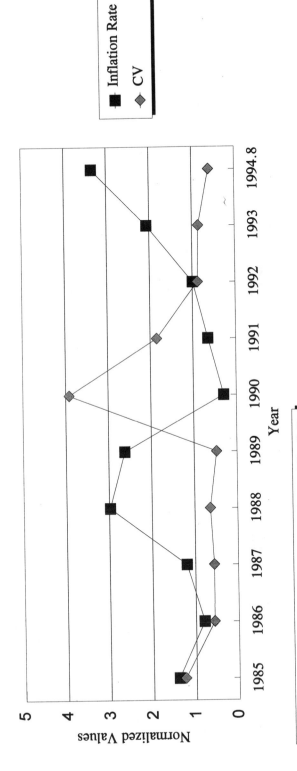

FIGURE 6
CV AND AVERAGE INFLATION RATE
(PROVINCE)

The units on Y-axis are normalized values. The S.D. for two sereis are 6.90 and 0.25, respectively.

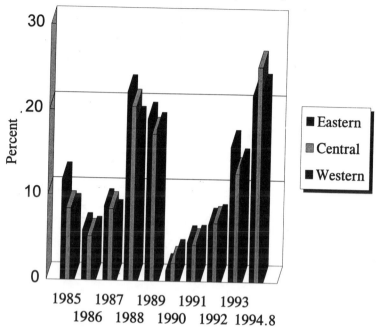

FIGURE 7A
AVERAGE INFLATION RATES(REGIONS)

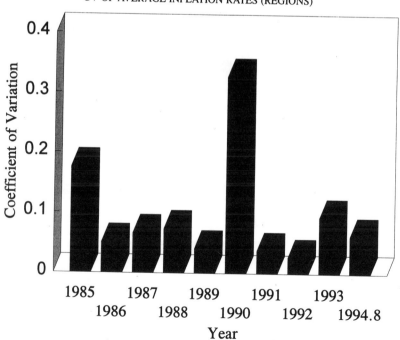

FIGURE 7B
CV OF AVERAGE INFLATION RATES (REGIONS)

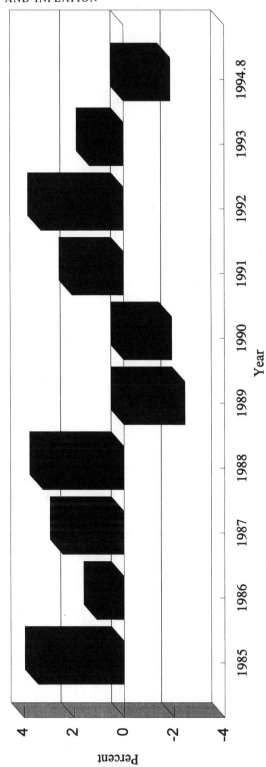

FIGURE 8
URBAN-RURAL INFLATION DIFFERENTIAL AVERAGE
(PROVINCE)

FIGURE 9
INFLATION, PROFIT GROWTH RATE, AND PRODUCTION COST GROWTH RATE

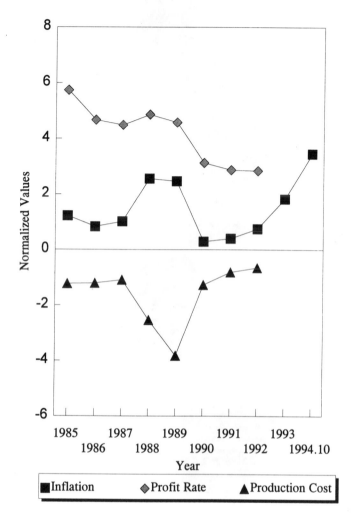

IMPACT ON INVESTMENT AND BUSINESS ENVIRONMENT

Inflation: Production Cost and Profitability, and Domestic and Foreign Investment

To see the co-movement of inflation with the growth rates of profits and production costs, the normalized values of the three series can be plotted comparatively (Figure 9). Production costs can be defined as the percentage decrease of the production costs of comparable products.[29] Therefore, a negative growth value in fact means an increase in the cost of production. The growth rate in the cost of production does follow the trend of the inflation rate. In fact, both have shown a negative correlation. When

FIGURE 10
INFLATION, NATIONAL INCOME GROWTH RATE, AND GDP GROWTH RATE

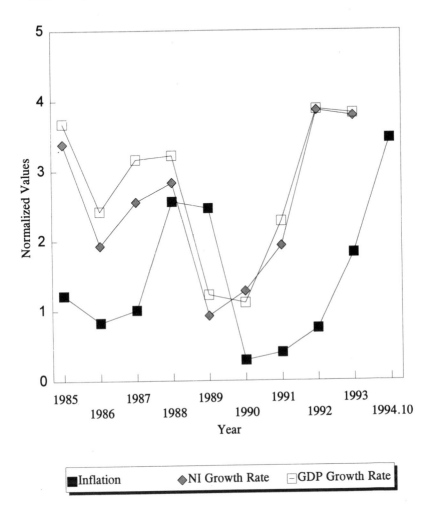

inflation was low, between 1985 and 1987, the growth rate of production cost was only between -6.7 and -7.5 per cent. Furthermore, when inflation was high in 1988 and 1989, the growth rate of the cost of production had soared to -15.5 and -23.4 per cent. Although the data for the cost of production only goes up to 1992,[30] it is reasonable to believe that the cost of production rose rather rapidly in 1993 and 1994, since its trend was so closely correlated with the rate of inflation up to 1992. With respect to the growth rate of profits, the figure shows that, before 1990, its trend has also very much followed the rate of inflation. However, having entered the 1990s, although the rate of inflation continued to rise, the growth rate of profits, at least up to 1992, was found to be declining. In fact, the growth rate of profits has been falling since 1979.[31] In other words, regardless of the inflation rate, the recent trend of the growth rate of profits has been a declining one. Since profit is the difference between total revenue and total cost, with the growth rate of the cost of production expected to be rising rapidly, the chance of a continuing falling trend in the growth rate of profits after 1992 is rather high.[32]

FIGURE 11
INFLATION, TOTAL DOMESTIC INVESTMENT GROWTH RATE, SIGNED FOREIGN
INVESTMENT GROWTH RATE, AND UTILIZED FOREIGN INVESTMENT GROWTH RATE

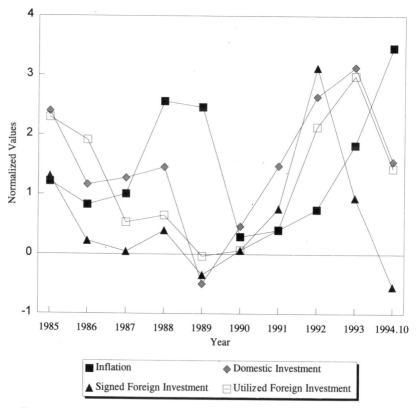

From a look at the inflation rate, together with the growth rates of national income and GDP, it can easily be construed that, between 1985 and 1992, the trend of the two growth rates is very much like the trend of inflation (Figure 10). The most interesting finding is that, taking a one year time-lag into account, the three trends demonstrate a similar pattern. This means that, within a half year time-lag, the growth rates of GDP and national income have strict positive correlations with inflation. They are so closely correlated that one must question the real meaning of China's GDP. Is GDP growth or decline inflated or deflated primarily or solely by inflation? Although the answer to this question is beyond this paper, evidently inflation does have a very significant impact on GDP.

The impact of inflation on investment can be clearly seen if the inflation rate is plotted together with the growth rates of total domestic investment, signed foreign investment, and utilized foreign investment (see Figure 11). The growth rates of the three investments closely follow the trend of inflation up to 1992. Since then, the rate of inflation, as mentioned earlier, has continued to increase. However, the growth rate of signed foreign investment fell in 1993, and the growth rates of the other two investments followed suit in 1994. The growth rate of signed foreign investment dropped from 254.1 to 76.8 per cent in 1993, and then further down to -44 per cent in October 1994.[33] For domestic investment, growth rate dropped from 50.6 to 25 per cent in 1994, while the one for utilized foreign investment dropped from 91.7 to 44 per cent. These figures, therefore, give full support to our suggestion that inflation has weakened the faith of investors, both domestic and foreign. In fact, inflation has a more direct and serious effect on the stability of the currency, in terms of the foreign exchange rate, which, in turn, has more a straightforward and critical impact on attracting foreign investment.[34] High inflation, particularly in an out-of-control state, will seriously destabilize the currency, taking the form of depreciation against foreign currencies, which, as a result, will severely damage both the confidence of overseas investors and the return rate of their investment.[35] The radical drop of signed foreign investment in 1994 is a clear illustration of how rampant Chinese inflation in 1994 hit overseas confidence and investment.

Disparities, Economic Development, and Administrative Disintegration

Extreme social and spatial inequalities are always major sources of social and political unrest that in turn can directly threaten the stability of the society and the disintegration of governmental administration.[36] Spatial disparities are an overall indication of, and comprehensive result of, uneven distribution of economic returns, development opportunities, and production capacities.[37] The uneven distribution of economic returns, caused mostly by a distorted price system which over-prices consumer goods or final products and under-prices producer goods or semi-products, is a 'greenhouse' for localism and territorial protectionism.[38] Long-term concentration on only one side of the country will certainly spur local political discontent and resistance, or even a rebellious attitude towards the central leadership.[39] The worst political, social, and economic consequences will result when these two uneven distributions combine and reinforce each other, acting against the poorer areas and regions.[40] What is more, adding insult to injury, these consequences are exacerbated by the prevailing rampant inflation, which, as discussed earlier, is mainly initiated by the richer regions but borne mostly by the poorer regions. This is exactly what has been happening in China since 1990. Widespread and active localism and the weakening of central influence and control have already caused political tension in China to reach an alarming level.[41] This condition is proved by those recent fiats in which the Chinese supreme party and central government have frequently called for 'united thoughts' and 'adhering to the central leadership'.[42] Therefore, it is not surprising to see that Beijing has recently been asking the top cadres in each province and in major cities to profess allegiance to the 'leadership collective with Jiang as its core'.[43] In addition, Beijing has also been trying to implement a rotating personnel system for top provincial leaders, so as to prevent army officers being drawn into an anti-Beijing coalition with local officials.[44] However, even with all these efforts, inflation still seems to be out of control (averaging about 25 per cent in October 1994), and, what is worse, as evidenced in China's most recent pivotal 'National Work Meeting' on the economy that was held in late 1994, the Chinese government still does not have any workable solution to the problem.[45]

INFLATION AND INEQUALITY IN AND BEYOND THE 1990s

Inflation: Up and Down

The current inflation in China is fundamentally different from the kind of inflation in any market economy.[46] The cause of this Chinese inflation is 'administrative failure' rather than market failure.[47] Unlike the kind caused by the malfunction of the invisible hand of market forces, inflation in China is by and large caused by the government, both central and local, and the visible hand of planning. There are three main causes for Chinese inflation: overheated investment, structural change, and inefficiency of state enterprises.[48] While overheated investment is largely blamed as the major fuel of inflation, the government is widely criticized for creating all three causes.

First, investment in China, except that funded by foreigners, comes mainly from four areas: government budgets, both central and local, bank loans and credits, state enterprises, and private enterprises and individuals. Except for the last category, these sources of investment are either directly controlled, or strongly influenced by, central and local governments.[49] Banks in China, no matter whether central or functional and sectoral, have their local affiliations controlled by the government at all administrative levels, including professional management and personnel appointments.[50] Since government approval is always required for any significant and new investment project, the investments of enterprises are also monitored by the government. Given the fact that the first three categories of investment comprise the major batch of total investment in China (state enterprises and bank loans have claimed 65–70 per cent and 20–30 per cent, respectively, of total social investment in fixed assets in recent years), their irrational increases will definitely create high inflation (Table 1). Therefore, the overheated investment, compounded by excessive money printing and bank credit, was obviously the main cause of high inflation in 1985, 1988 to 1989, and 1993 to the present.[51] On the other hand, the current rampant inflation, which soared to 25 per cent in October 1994, was also fueled by 42–50 per cent growth in domestic investment and 66–92 per cent growth in foreign utilized investment between 1992 and 1993 (Table 1).

Second, the prevailing high inflation is also the result of structual change, the change from a traditional to a more modern economy.[52] This type of structural change requires a series adjustment across sectors (primary, secondary, and tertiary) and industries (basic/heavy and consumer/light) through the manoeuvering of their corresponding prices. Under the long-term misrule of China's administrative mechanism, production and the supply of raw materials, energy, agricultural products, and transportation have proved to be bottlenecks for economic growth. Thus, the price increases of these goods, in the form of either official price raising or market determination, have in fact been unavoidable. This structural change was, therefore, the cause of the inflation that existed in 1980–84 and in 1993–94, when prices of agricultural products, fuel, and raw materials, all increased by 50–100 per cent (Table 1).[53] However, after 15 years of economic reforms and development, the problem of sectoral mismatch not only remains unresolved, but has become even worse. Given that government still controls and influences a large part of social investment, the under-development of agriculture, basic industries, and infrastructure is in fact the consequence of the administrative mistakes committed by the government.

TABLE 1

COMPREHENSIVE SOCIAL AND ECONOMIC INDICATORS IN CHINA: 1985–93

Year	1985	1986	1987	1988	1989	1990	1991	1992	1993	94.10*
Retail Price Index	8.8	6	7.3	18.5	17.8	2.1	2.9	5.4	13.2	25
CV of Percapita GDP	0.72	0.71	0.69	0.67	0.64	0.63	0.64	0.67		
CV of Personal Income	0.16	0.17	0.18	0.18	0.19	0.19	0.21	0.22		
PretaxesProfit/ Fixed Assets	24.8	20.2	19.4	21	19.8	13.5	12.4	12.3		
Comparable Production	-7.5	-7.4	-6.7	-15.5	-23.4	-7.8	-5.0	-4.0		
National Income Growth	13.5	7.7	10.2	11.3	3.7	5.1	7.7	15.4	15.1	
GDP Growth Rate	12.9	8.5	11.1	11.3	4.3	3.9	8	13.6	13.4	
Total Investment Growth	38.7	18.8	20.6	23.5	-8.0	7.5	23.8	42.6	50.6	20
Signed Foreign Investment	106.3	18.2	3.4	32.2	-28.1	5.2	62.0	254.1	76.8	-44
Utilized Foreign Investment	70.4	58.7	16.4	20.0	-1.0	2.0	12.6	65.5	91.7	44

*Data from Smith New Court Far East Ltd., a HK-based consultancy firm, which is verified by various newspapers, including *RMRB*.

Source: Processed from China's Statistical Yearbook: 1985–94.

Third, inefficiency of state enterprises is another key reason for inflation.[54] Out of all the production units, the operation of the state economy is the least efficient.[55] While the compatible production cost has been increasing since the beginning of the urban reforms, the pre-tax profit rate of state enterprises has been declining (Table 1 and Figure 9). Currently, one third of state enterprises are running an open deficit and another one third are running at a concealed deficit (where the financial account is balanced only due to government subsidies).[56] The inefficiency of state enterprises not only uses up a substantial part of government fiscal revenue but also contributes greatly to inflation.

The administrative nature of inflation in China is reflected not only in the cause of inflation, but also in the way that inflation is curbed. Instead of using instruments such as changing the interest rate or altering the reserve ratio, the way the Chinese government controls inflation is purely through an austerity policy, which is virtually equal to giving administrative orders only.[57] Under so-called 'Chinese socialist characteristics', such administrative orders will bring forward no bankruptcy of state enterprises, no structural adjustment, no resource and investment optimization, and no improvement in production efficiency. The austerity policy simply means 'stop and go' orders.[58] Inflation that is contained during the 'stop' period will accumulate and be intensified in the next 'go' period. Therefore, under the often switching 'stop and go' administrative regime, a vicious economic cycle of boom and bust continues and further intensifies.

As acknowledged by Ma Kai, a Vice-Minister of the State Commission for Restructuring the Economic System of the PRC, in his speech in a Conference in UK,[59] the deadlock of Chinese inflation is administrative failure and the underlying platform of this failure, as discussed earlier, is the state economy and state ownership of the means of production.[60] After 15 years of reforms, the relationships between government and enterprises are, unfortunately, not much changed, or even worse. The government, particularly the local one, has become unprecendently 'authoritarian' and has even more vested interests in the economy. So far, state enterprise reforms have made no meaningful progress in improving this relationship and a real breakthrough is nowhere in sight.[61] Although the Party and top leaders of the government all vowed in the most recent 'National Working Meeting on the Economy' that some 'major strides' in enterprise reforms will take place in 1995, at the same time they also ruled out the possibilities of privatization, massive bankruptcies, and large-scale conversion of state enterprises into sharing companies.[62] Therefore, 'waiting to die' seems to be the fate of all Chinese state enterprises.

Meaningful reform of the government role in both state enterprises and the economy is currently impossible.[63] Given the peculiar administrative features of the Chinese economy and inflation, and the experience of reforms during the last 15 years, it can be reasonably forseen that China's inflation, an endless administrative game or vicious planning circle, will continue to fluctuate, and its magnitude will be intensified and its cycle will shorten in the next five to 10 years.

FIGURE 12
RELATIVE DISPERSION OF PROVINCIAL NMP PER CAPITA (CURRENT PRICES)

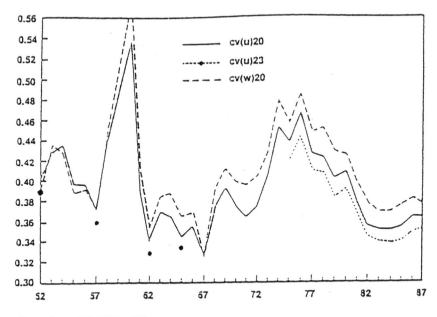

Source: Lyons, T.P. (1991), p.476

Disparities and Localism: Intensifying

Serious regional inequalities are only just beginning, and a full-gear drive
of spatial disparities, compounded by an upsurge in localism/territorial
protectionism, will be seen in the next five to ten years. The first rationale
that underpins the above argument is that spatial disparities of per capita
GDP, real consumption per capita, and real income per capita have, for the
first time ever, all began to shoot in the same direction and upwards since
1990. Analyzing the recent trends of these disparities reveals an interesting
and important finding: disparity of GDP went in the opposite direction to
those of consumption and income before 1990, but has moved in the same
direction since then (Figures 12 and 13). That is, while the CVs of
consumption per capita and real income per capita have started to rise since
the mid 1980s, the CV of per capita GDP declined continuously from the
mid 1970s till the end of the 1980s and that trend has only been reversed
since 1990.[64] In other words, the upward trends of the disparities of
consumption and income were partially offset by the downward trend of the
disparity of production before 1990 (Figure 12 and Figure 13). This
phenonmenon no doubt tempered the exacerbation of consumption and
income disparities in the 1980s.[65]

However, this counteracting force appears to have disappeared since
1990. For this reason, one can responsibly argue that some real and serious
inter-regional disparities have just been began to form in China, and that they

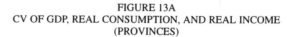

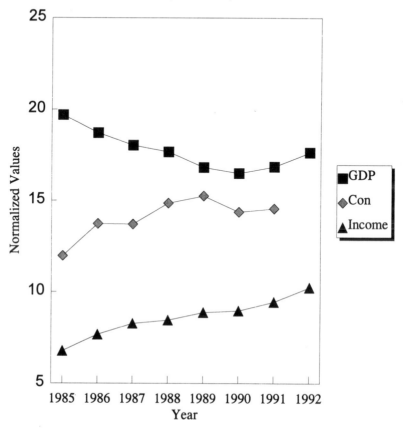

FIGURE 13A
CV OF GDP, REAL CONSUMPTION, AND REAL INCOME
(PROVINCES)

The units on Y-axis are normalized values.
The S.D. of the three sereis are 0.63, 0.02, and 0.21, respectively.

will run at full gear at least until early 2000. The disparities of consumption and income that have suddenly changed direction and began at an increasing rate since 1990 to support our argument (Figure 3C, 4B, and 5B).

The second rationale that underpins our argument is based on the distribution of Chinese total investment in the last decade. In addition to supporting our general argument, this second rationale will also give support to our first argument. However, before presenting this second reason, it is necessary to review first the spatial policy of China during the 1980s and the early 1990s, as background material, as stated in Zhao. (1996)[66]:

> For the whole of the 1980s, China's spatial strategy was dominated by Deng's 'get rich first' principle and the 'Coastal Development Strategy', which were endorsed in the Party's conference and The State's Sixth Five-Year Plan (FYP) in 1980. In the conference and the

FIGURE 13B
CV OF GDP, REAL CONSUMPTION, AND REAL INCOME
(REGIONS)

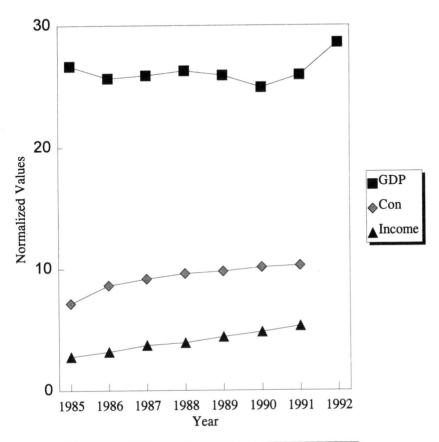

The units on Y-axis are normalized values.
The S.D. of the three sereis are 0.013, 0.019, and 0.022, respectively.

sixth FYP, the Party and the government for the first-time ever frankly
and boldly recognized the inevitability that a widening inequality was
a short-term consequence of rapid economic development. As a result,
four special economic zones (Shenzhen, Zhuhai, Shantou, and
Xiamen) were set up (in 1980), followed by the wide-ranging
establishment of fourteen open coastal port cities, three open
economic regions in the major river deltas (in 1984–85), and the new
special province of Hainan Island (in 1988) in the coastal region. In
addition, a series of special (favorable and preferential) policies in
decision-making, finance, investment and foreign trade, as well as in
central and overseas fund allocation, were set up swiftly one after
another for the coastal regions.

In the mid-1980s, due to wide-spread localism, such as competing/fighting and blockading for natural resources and commodity markets, the Seventh Five-Year Plan[67] appealed for labour division and spatial specialization and cooperation. However, this blue print was soon replaced by Zhao Ziyang's 'Coastal development strategy',[68] which stressed giving more power to the coastal regions and letting them join the global economic circle with both material supplies and markets overseas. This strategy was formally endorsed by the Party's conference in early 1988 and since then China's east coastal development priorties have become the most momentous recent phenomenon. It has even become the Party's political mobilization strategy.

Entering the 1990s, wide-spread complaints and discontent from the interior regions, and social concerns for equality, forced Li Peng's government to pay attention to the problems of spatial inequality for the first time. His government report[69] and the government's Eighth Five-Year-Plan and Ten-Year-Planning for the 1990s[70] was revised substantially by the delegates in the People's Congress Conference in 1990. The result was the final adoption of some policies favoring interior development, such as introducing 'open door policies' to interior provinces, so-called 'Open up in all direction', and the more vigorous setting up of a package of 'relief and assistance to poor and minority provinces and regions'.[71] However, this national policy appears to have remained at the rhetorical level, since data shows that national investment shifted even more radically toward the east coastal regions in early 1990s (see later discussion). The east coastal priority policy and development momentum remained unchanged.'

A detailed examination of the distribution of both domestic and foreign investment in the past decade in China can at best reflect the spatial priority of national development and explain the disparities caused by that development. Figure 14 A (regional shares) and B (provincial and regional CVs) and Table 2 (foreign investment) summarize the distribution features of both domestic and foreign investments in China. The overall picture is that coastal domination in receiving both domestic and foreign investments is too evident and overwhelming. In particular, foreign investment in the eastern region, which is usually under central regulation,[72] accounted for 93 per cent in 1979–89 and 87 per cent 1989–92. Along with this overall picture, there is also another interesting and important finding. A sharp rise in domestic investment in the eastern region, in terms of both eastern share (Figure 14A) and provincial and regional CVs (Figure 14 B), took place in 1985 and has been accelerating since then. This is understandable since it was in 1985 that China launched its urban reforms and opened its vast coastal cities and regions to foreign investment. As a result, 'the east coastal development strategy' was heralded and became fully operational. Although the CVs of investment in 1991 dropped from their peak of

1989–90, they again returned to their peak level in 1992 (Figure14B). However, during the period 1985–90, China's disparities of both provincial and regional GDP did not rise but declined, at the same time as the disparities (CVs) of both private consumption and personal income soared (Figure 13). This can be reasonably explained by the fact that any economic returns or the effects of investments in large-scale production and infrastructure projects usually take five to ten years, while the time lag for the consumption effects of investments is usually six months to one year (the increase of personal cash income and consumption almost immediately follows the time when the investments are put into use). The declined disparities in economic output in the 1980s were caused by the general effects of economic reform and the Party's 'economic works' launched in 1979, which made development 'a national phenomenon' and helped to bring down the higher degree of disparity produced in Mao's periods.[73]

TABLE 2
DISTRIBUTIONS OF UTILIZED FOREIGN INVESTMENTS IN CHINA: 1979-1992
(PERCENTAGE BY REGION)

	1979–88	1989–92	1993 (est.)
Eastern Region	92.8	84.7	increased
(Guangdong)	(58.8)	(38.0)	increased
Central Region	meaningless	6.9	decreased
Western Region	meaningless	4.0	decreased

Note: In 1993, China attracted actual or utilized foreign investment of US$26bn, while contractual investment was US$100bn, equivalent to the total promised in the thirteen years previously.
Source: Zhao, Xiaobin (1996), 'Spatial disparities of economic development in China - a time-series of comparative studies', Development and Change, Vol.27, No.1.

However, since entering the 1990s, these general economic effects have been offset by the accumulated effects of excessive investment in the eastern regions over the last ten years, particularly over the last five years from 1985. Moreover, adding insult in injury, another sharp and disproportional shift of investment toward the eastern region and greater disparities (CVs) has once again taken place since 1991 (Figure 14A and B and Table 2). That is why this paper argues that a serious regional inequality and disparity have only just begun and that more exacerbated and intensified disparities will be seen later in the 1990s and beyond. Considering the 'five to ten year-span' that large-scale investment takes to produce actual effects and the further concentration of investment in the eastern regions in the early 1990s, the pattern of exacerbated and intensified disparities will not change for the next five to ten years. There is no doubt that the massive investments, both foreign and domestic, in the last five to ten years have formed real and overwhelming advantages in infrastructure, production capacity, and modern technology in the eastern region. From

FIGURE 14A
REGIONAL SHARES OF TOTAL INVESTMENT IN FIXED ASSETS

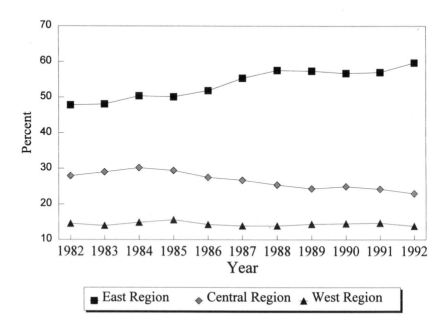

now on these advantages, combined with the accumulative and causation effects of market forces,[74] will enter a high peak period and will fully play out their roles over the next five to ten years. This pattern will not change even if the central government immediately takes action, say in the next five-year period (1996-2000), to prevent it. However, the current central government so far seems to have no intention of doing so. Furthermore, even it has, it is also very much in doubt whether the central government has the ability to do so, both politically and fiscally.

CONCLUSION

This paper has examined the recent trends, impacts and projections of spatial inequalities and the spatiality of inflation in China. The findings in this paper suggest that China's spatial inequality, in terms of inter-provincial and inter-regional production (GDP) and distribution (private comsuption and personal income), has deteriorated severely, particularly since 1990. China is also an extraordinarily unequal country, in terms of urban-rural income differential/ratio, by the standard of other developing countries of

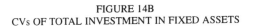

FIGURE 14B
CVs OF TOTAL INVESTMENT IN FIXED ASSETS

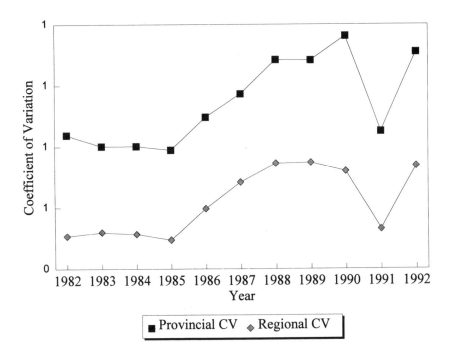

Asia.[75] What is more, this inequality gap is still enlarging. The worst thing is that the current steep rise in regional inequality of economic development and income distribution has been compounded and exacerbated by inflation, which appears to be both enduring and spatially very foot-loose and, thus, hits poorer areas disproportionately harder.

Given the fact that alternation of the current trends of inequality is almost impossible in the short run, and a thorough medicine which can cure Chinese inflation at its deep roots is also nowhere in sight; therefore, a mutual reinforcement of both disparity and inflation and its induced upsurge of rampant localism will be seen for the coming five to ten years. Thus, China's investment and business environment in the 1990s, in terms of both political and social unrest and economic profitability, will be severely undermined and will, therefore, become increasingly uncertain. This tendency seems likely to continue, accelerated and exacerbated until the early part of the next century. In the next five to ten years, Chinese prosperity and stability, business environments, economic reforms, the central authority, as well as the whole 'socialist' system will face real challenges, and the resultant consequences will be hard to predict.

ACKNOWLEDGEMENTS

An earlier version of this paper was presented at the '94 Annual Conference of The Chinese Economic Association (UK) in LSE, London on 14–15 December 1994. The authors thank the participants in the conference for their valuable criticisms. Special gratitude is due to Chow Siutin for his invaluable help in assembling materials and to Qu Hong Bin and his working company (Smith New Court Far East Ltd) for providing the most up-to-date data.

APPENDIX

Letting y_i represent GDP per capita in area i, and n the number of areas, define

$$\bar{y} \equiv \frac{\sum_{i=1}^{n} \bar{y}_i}{n}$$

The coefficient of variation is

$$CV(n) \equiv \frac{\sqrt{\sum_{i=1}^{n} (y_i - \bar{y})^2 / n}}{\bar{y}}$$

The coefficient of variation is a measure of relative dispersion, i.e., of dispersion relative to the mean. Its numerator is the standard deviation – the most often used measure of absolute dispersion. To see the range of a variable, it is more useful to look at the standardized difference. Using the same notation, the standardized difference is

$$Std \ Diff \equiv \frac{Max(y)}{Min(y)}$$

Standardized difference is an efficient measure to compare the most well-off with the least.

NOTES

1. See Aguignier, P. 'Regional disparities since 1978', in Feuchtwang, S. *et al.* (eds) (1988) *Transforming China's Economy in the Eighties: the Urban sector,* Vol.2, (London: Zed Books Ltd., 1988), pp.93–106; Cannon, T. 'Regions: Spatial Inequality and Regional Policy', in Cannon, T. and Jenkins, A. (eds) (1990) *The Geography of Contemporary China* (London and New York: Routledge, 1990), pp.28–60 ; Falkenheim, V.C., 'Spatial Inequality in China's Modernization Program: Some Political–Administrative Determinants', in Leung, C.K. and Chai, C.H. (eds) *Development and Distribution in China,* (Hong Kong: University of Hong Kong, 1995); Goodman, D.G. (ed) *China's Regional Development,* (London: Routledge, 1989); Lakshmanan, T.R. and Chang, I.H., 'Regional Disparities in China', *International Regional Science Review,* Vol.11, No.1 (1987), pp.97–103; Lo, Chor-Pang, 'The Geography of Rural Regional Inequality in Mainland China', *Transactions of the Institute of British Geographers,* Vol.15, No.4 (1990) , pp.466–86; Naughton, B., 'The Third Tront: Defence Industrialization in the Chinese Interior', *The China Quarterly* Vol.115 (1988) , pp.351–86; Paine, S., 'Spatial Aspects of Chinese Development – Issues, Outcomes and Policies, 1949–79', *Journal of Development Studies,* Vol.17, No.1 (1981), pp.132–95; Pannell, C., 'Regional Shifts in China's industrial output', *Professional Geographer, Vol.*40, No.1 (1988), pp.19–32.; Yang, Dali, 'Patterns of China's Regional Development Strategy', *The China Quarterly,* Vol. 122, No.2 (1990), pp.230–57; Zhao, Xiaobin, 'Reforms and Regional Inequality in China:1953–89', *China Report,* Vol.30, No.3 (1994a), pp.331–43.

2. Both studies focus on time-series comparison of spatial inequalities during Mao's traditional and Deng's reform regimes. Lyons (1991) focues on the trend of interprovincial inequality which prevailed in 1953–87, while Zhao (1996), in a more comprehensive capacity and up-to-date data input, provides an in-depth account of why Mao's interior development (1953–78) had not led to a more equitable outcome than Deng's seemingly uneven strategy of 'east coastal development' (1979–90). See Zhao, Xiaobin, 'Spatial Disparities and Economic Development in China: Comparative Studies', *Development and Change,* Vol.27, No.1 (1996), pp.131–63 and Lyons, 'Interprovincial Disparities in China', *Economic Development and Cultural Change,* Vol.39, No.1 (1991), pp.471–506.

3. Khan *et al.* provides a striking features of the composition of household income, which differs from the SSB survey and its distribution, based on their own survey of 10,258 rural households and 9,009 urban households in 10 provinces in 1987, while Chai C.H. focuses on inequalites on the comsumption side, based on data from SSB's China'S Statistical Year-books. See Khan, A.R., K. Griffin, C. Riskin, and R.W. Zhao, 'Household Income and its Distribution in China', *The China Quarterly,* Vol. 132 (1992), pp.1029–61; Chai , C. H., 'Consumption and Living Standards in China', *The China Quarterly,* Vol.131 (1992), pp.721–49

4. These include most of the studies in footnotes 1, 2 and 3.

5. The authors, based in Hong Kong and originating from mainland China, have recently been asked this question by HK-based businessmen and consultancy firms, at both private and formal occasions, such as consultancy talks and interviews by public media.

6. See Lardy, N.R. 'Consumption and Living Standards in China, 1978–83', in *The China Quarterly,* Vol. 100, pp.849–65 (1984); Khan, A.R., K. Griffin, C. Riskin, and R.W. Zhao, 'Household Income and its Distribution in China'; Chai , C.H., 'Consumption and Living Standards in China', and Zhao, Xiaobin and Zhang L., 'Urbanization and Urban Policy on City-size in China', *Urban Studies,* Vol.35, No.5 (1995).

7. See Khan, A.R., K. Griffin, C. Riskin, and R.W. Zhao, 'Household Income and its Distribution in China', pp.1034–7.

8. Ibid., p.1035.

9. Ibid., p.1037.

10. Interview with the officals of SSB, with which the author (Zhao X.) used to have close working relations.

11. See Lyons,'Interprovincial Disparities in China'; Chai , C.H., 'Consumption and Living Standards in China', and Zhao, Xiaobin, 'Reforms and Regional Inequality in China:1953–89'; and Chai , C.H., 'Consumption and Living Standards in China'.

12. See Khan, A.R., K. Griffin, C. Riskin, and R.W. Zhao, 'Household Income and its Distribution in China.'

13. This means that distribution of these two incomes among people or social groups does not vary much across places/provinces.

14. See Khan, A.R., K. Griffin, C. Riskin, and R.W. Zhao, 'Household Income and its Distribution in China,' p.1037.

15. See Zhao, Xiaobin, 'Rapid Economic Growth and Backward Infrastructure and Social Development : A Case Study in Guangdong', *Asian Studies,* Vol.11 (1994b), pp.166–86 and Zhao, Xiaobin and Zhang L., 'Urbanization and Urban Policy on City-size in China', *Urban Studies,* Vol.35, No.5 (1995).

16. This analysis simply cannot to be done using its own survey and data sampling.

17. The net material product (NMP) per capita or the national income per capita was used as an indicator in this study. However, its results or implications on spatial disparity are mostly the same as the per capita GDP; therefore, it will not be reported here.

18. Data for the 1994 inflation rate was provided by a Hong Kong-based international consultant firm: Smith New Court Far East Ltd, and was verified by Remin Ribao (People's Daily) during early 1995.

19. See Lyons,'Interprovincial Disparities in China' and Zhao, 'Spatial Disparities and Economic Development in China.'

20. Data on per capita consumption is available only up to 1991. Therefore, our investigation on spatial disparity, when indicated by real consumption per capita, will cover only the period from 1985 to 1991.

21. The provinces included in the eastern region are Beijing, Shanghai, Tianjin, Hebei, Liaoling,

Shandong, Jiangsu, Zhejiang, Guangdong, Fujian, Hainan, and Guangxi. The central region consists of Anhui, Hubei, Heilongjian, Jiangxi, Jilin, Shanxi, Neimongol, Hunan, and Henan. The western region consists of Sichuan, Guizhou, Yunan, Qinghai, Gansu, Shaanxi, Ningxia, Xinjiang, and Xizang. For rationales for this division see Lu, Dadao, (ed) *Maps of Chinese Industrial Distribution*, (Beijing:China Planning Press, 1987) and Lu, Dadao, 'The East–West Change of China's industrial location', *Shengchan Buju yu Guotu Guihua* (Productive Location and Territorial Management), Vol.8 (1988), pp.14–24.

22. In fact, the authors have also calculated the Gini-coefficiency for all the indicators used in the paper. However, the results are similar to the CV. So only CV is used and presented in this paper.
23. To put two series in the same figure, we have normalized the values of each series by its corresponding standard deviation.
24. See Lyons,'Interprovincial Disparities in China', p.505.
25. In Fig. 3C, the observations for 1FYP, 2FYP, and so on, are all average values – each represents the average of five years. FYP stands for five-year plan and thus 1FYP is the average urban–rural household consumption differential for the five years included in the first five-year plan. 3ADJ stands for the average of the adjustment period (1963 to 1965).
26. Here, real income means real income per capita.
27. This is the ratio of urban to rural income, rural figure is as 1.
28. See Khan, A. R., K. Griffin, C. Riskin, and R.W. Zhao, 'Household Income and its Distribution in China', p.1037.
29. See Liu, Zinan and Liu, Guy Shaajia, ' The Efficiency Impact of Chinese Industrial Reform in the 1980s', '*94 Conference Paper of the Chinese Economic Association in the UK*, No.94004 (The Chinese Economic Association in the U.K, 1994)
30. The latest Data from BBS ZGTJNJ (1994)
31. See Liu, Guoguang, *80 Niandai Zhongguo Jingji Gaige Yu Fazhan* [China's Economic Reform and Development in 1980s], (Beijing: Jingji Guanli Press, 1991a); Li, Yining, *Zhongguo Jingji Gaige De Silu* [Thoughts on Chinese Reform], (Beijing: Zhongguo Zhanwang Chubanshe [China Prospect Press], 1989a)
32. See Liu, Zinan and Liu, Guy Shaajia, 'The Efficiency Impact of Chinese Industrial Reform in the 1980s'.
33. The growth rates are all in terms of last year, that is, a 254.1 means the growth rate of investment this year is 254.1% of last year.
34. For details see Luo, Qi and Howe, C., 'Direct Investment and Economic Integration in the Asia Pacific: The Case of Taiwanese Investment in Xiamen', *The China Quarterly*, Vol.136 (1994), pp.746–69.
35. Ibid.
36. See Falkenheim, V.C., 'Spatial Inequality in China's Modernization Program: Some Political–Administrative Determinants', in Leung, C.K. and Chai, C.H. (eds) *Development and Distribution in China*; Solinger, D., 'Uncertain Paternalism: Tensions in Recent Regional Restructuring in China', *International Regional Science Review*, Vol.11, No.1 (1987), pp.23–43; Wong, P.W., 'Fiscal Reform and Local Industrialization', *Modern China*, Vol.18, No.2 (1992), pp.197–227.
37. See Gilbert, A.G. (ed.) *Development Planning and Spatial Structure* (London: John Wiley, 1976) and Zhao Xiaobin, *Systemic Restructuring for Regional Development in China* (PhD Thesis, University of Manchester, 1992).
38. See Markusen, A.R. *Politics of Regions: the Economics and Politics of Territory* (Totowa: Rowman & Littlefield, 1987) and Zhao, Xiaobin and Kwan, W., 'The Relationships between the Central and Local Governments and their Impact on Regional Development in China'.
39. Ibid.
40. Ibid.
41. See *South China Mornning Post (SCMP)*, June 12 1994.
42. See *Renmin Ribao (RMRB)* December 12 1994.
43. See *China Daily* December 2 1994.
44. See *SCMP* December 6 1994.
45. The conference, sponsored by the Central Committee of the Party and the State Council, had set four major tasks for 1995: curbing inflation, boosting agriculture, reforming state enterprises, and strengthening central government controls. Attended by most party and government top leaders, the conference had President Jiang Zemin, Premier Li Peng, and

Vice-premier Zhu Rongji as the keynote speakers.

46. See Qin, Duo, 'Explanation and Prediction of the Inflationary Process during China 's Economic Reforms', 94' Conference Paper of the Chinese Economic Association in the UK, No.94001 (the Chinese Economic Association in the UK 1994); Wu, Jinglian, 'The Plan and Market', and Liu, Guoguang, *Gaige. Wending. Fazhan* [Economic Reform, Stabilization, and Development], (Beijing: Jingji Guanli Press, 1991b).

47. See Zhao Xiaobin, *Systemic Restructuring for Regional Development in China.*

48. See Wu, Jinglian, 'The Plan and Market', and Liu, Guoguang, *Gaige. Wending. Fazhan* [Economic Reform, Stabilization, and Development], (Beijing: Jingji Guanli Press, 1991b).

49. Wu, Jinglian, 'The Plan and Market', and Liu, Guoguang, *Gaige. Wending. Fazhan* [Economic Reform, Stabilization, and Development].

50. See Selden, M., *The Political Economy of Contemporary China*, (Armonk: N.Y., Sharpe, 1988) and Selden, M., *The Political Economy of Chinese Development*, (Armonk: N.Y., Sharpe, 1993).

51. Wu, Jinglian, 'The Plan and Market', and Liu, Guoguang, *Gaige. Wending. Fazhan* [Economic Reform, Stabilization, and Development].

52. Ibid.

53. Ma, Kai, 'China's Economic Situation and the Status Quo and Prospects of Reform', '94 Conference Paper of the Chinese Economic Association in the UK, No.94001 (the Chinese Economic Association in the UK, 1994).

54. Li, Yining, *Zhongguo Jingji Wang Hechuqu* [Where is the Chinese Economy Heading for?], (Hongkong:, Shangwu Yinshuguan Co. Ltd., 1989b).

55. See Liu, Zinan and Liu, Guy Shaajia, 'The Efficiency Impact of Chinese Industrial Reform in the 1980s'.

56. Li, (as note 54), and Liu, Guoguang, *Gaige. Wending. Fazhan (Economic Reform, Stabilization, and Development.*

57. Ibid.

58. Also see Qin, Duo, 'Explanation and Prediction of the Inflationary Process during China's Economic Reforms', 94' Conference Paper of The Chinese Economic Association in the U. K., No:94001 (The Chinese Economic Association in the U. K., 1994)

59. Ma Kai was invited as a keynote speeker and addressed on opening event of 94's Annual conference of The Chinese Economic Association in the UK. He acknowledged that excessive investment and money-printing and persistant 'bottle-necks' in basic sectors are the key reasons for the Chinese inflation, but 'The fundamental reason behind the repeated appearance of the strange cycle of ' expansion-retrenchment followed by another round expansion-etrenchment, ans so on...' lies in ....the old system'. See Ma , Kai, 'China's Economic Situation and the Status Quo and Prospects of Reform', pp1–3.

60. Also see Li, Yining, *Zhongguo Jingji Wang Hechuqu* [Where is the Chinese Economy Heading for?], and Zhao Xiaobin and Kwan, W., 'The Relationships between the Central and Local Government s and their Impact on Regional Development in China', (1994).

61. See Perry, E.J., 'Trends in the Study of Chinese Politics:State–Society Relations', *The China Quarterly*, Vol.139 (1994), pp.704–13 and Zhao Xiaobin, 'Rapid Economic Growth and Backward Infrastructure and Social Development: A Case Study in Guangdong ', *Asian Studies*, Vol.11 (1994b), pp.166–86.

62. See *SCMP*, 2 December 1994.

63. Selden, M., *The Political Economy of Chinese Development*, (Armonk: NY, Sharpe, 1993). and Perry, E.J., 'Trends in the Study of Chinese Politics:State–Society Relations', (1994)

64. For detailed explanations of these trends see Zhao, Xiaobin, 'Reforms and Regional Inequality in China: 1953–89'; Zhao, Xiaobin, 'Spatial Disparities of Economic Development in China – Time-Series of Comparative Studies'; and Lyons,'Interprovincial Disparities in China'.

65. Production or economic output does not equal distribution of income, but certainly relates and influences the outcome of distribution of income to some extent. For instance, producing more may lead to gaining more, if other conditions remain equal.

66. See Zhao, Xiaobin, 'Spatial Disparities of Economic Development in China – Time-Series of Comparative Studies'.

67. See *RMRB*, 26 September 1985.

68. Zhao, Ziyang, 'The Strategy of Economic Development in Coastal Regions' in *The State Economic System Reform Commission* (ed.) *Zhongguo Jinji Tizhi Gaige Shinian* [Ten Years

of Economic Reform as in China], (Beijing: Jinji Guanli Press and Gaige Press) (1988), pp.99–104.

69. See *RMRB*, 20 January 1991.
70. See *RMRB*, 16 April 1991.
71. See *RMRB*, 20 January 20 1991
72. See Zhao, Xiaobin, 'Reforms and Regional Inequality in China:1953–89'.
73. See Lyons,'Interprovincial Disparities in China'.
74. Myrdal, G., *Economic Theoy and Underdeveloped Regions*, (London:Duckworth, 1957).
75. See Khan, A.R., K. Griffin, C. Riskin, and R.W. Zhao, 'Household Income and its Distribution in China', p.1037.

Hermes Revisited: A Replication of Hofstede's Study in Hong Kong and the UK

SID LOWE

INTRODUCTION

Hofstede's well-known study of cross-cultural values has come to be regarded as amongst the most influential in the field,[1] and the subsequent extensive citation of a study, which involved the measurement of international differences in cultural values within IBM or 'Hermes', is testimony to its seminal status. Unfortunately, this success has not been matched by increased co-operative research amongst social scientists into cultural issues, namely through an 'intersubjective' approach which was one of Hofstede's hopes for subsequent development.[2] Hofstede's approach, based on the comparative explanation of work-related values, is categorized and labelled variously and using different typologies,[3] thus re-emphasizing that his approach is not the only perspective. Hofstede's support for an integration of social science approaches is based on the premise that subjectivity in social science is inevitable, since 'Man-the-social-scientist' is less complex than his object. The metaphor of the blind man from the Indian fable is used by Hofstede to signify a belief in the need for 'blind' social scientists to combine perspectives in order to improve understanding of their object. Hofstede thus pre-empts much of the criticism of his work by a priori recognizing its limitations, resulting from his own particular type of 'blindness'.

PURPOSE OF STUDY

This article, in replicating Hofstede's 1980 study within IBM (the original vehicle used by Hofstede, and called 'Hermes' by him) attempts to address concerns such as 'whether the country profiles identified by Hofstede are stable.'[4] Moreover, 'Hofstede speculates that the individualism index for a country will increase with the wealth of that country. More evidence collected over a long period of time is needed, however, before one can draw this conclusion.'[5] The main purpose is to examine the validity of Hofstede's Values Survey Module (VSM) within the original sampling organization, using matched samples in different countries as a way, therefore, to cross-validate the instrument and findings of the original study, as suggested in a recent review of Hofstede replications.[6] Such validation would justify arguments in favour of Hofstede's principal hypotheses that

Sid Lowe, King's College, London

management is culture-bound and that American and Western theories of management which dominate the literature are ethnocentric and mistakenly interpreted as universally applicable. The two countries used in this replication are Hong Kong and the UK These were chosen to examine cultural differences between a Western industrialized nation and a rapidly industrializing country in the Asia Pacific. There is no suggestion , however, that these countries are statistically 'representative' of their respective regions.

The structure of the article involves an initial review of the role of culture from different perspectives, followed by a summary of Hofstede's four dimensional (4-D) model and the addition of a fifth dimension following the contribution of 'The Chinese Culture Connection' in identifying an 'emic' (or culturally unique) Chinese dimension. Following a discussion of Hong Kong culture, critiques of Hofstede's model are reviewed and the details of the method and results of the replication are described and discussed. Finally, a summary is given and conclusions are drawn.

THE ROLE OF CULTURE

In describing and explaining culture we are faced with considerable difficulties resulting in a tendency for researchers to provide a selection of definitions which might best capture its essence.

Alternative Views of The Role of Culture

Seeing culture as a type of mental programming is reported by Triandis to be based upon the concept of socialization.[7] This, as with many other issues of culture, is not a universally accepted approach, as it reflects a structural-functional perspective which views culture as something a collective entity *has* rather than something a collective entity *is*.

Hofstede's Definitions of Culture

Definitions of culture range from the very broad to the very narrow, reflecting the extent to which culture permeates human experiences at different levels. Hofstede recognizes the levels of culture by providing a narrow and a broad definition.[8] The former concerns 'civilization' or 'refinement of the mind' and the concomitants of education, art and literature. The broader definition which is derived from social anthropology and deals with more fundamental human processes (including those within the narrow definition) is the main concern for Hofstede and also for this article. This broad definition is given as 'the collective programming of the mind which distinguishes the members of one group or category of people from another.'[9]

Levels of 'Mental Programmes' and Difficulties in Interpretation

Values are defined by Hofstede as 'a broad tendency to prefer certain states of affairs over others.'[10] Values are attributes of individuals and collectivities (Hofstede refers to *norms* in the latter case). They are non-rational but determine our 'subjective definition of rationality.'[11] Values have both intensity and direction, and they are distinguishable between the *desired* (phenomenological) and the *desirable* (deontological). Hofstede warns against the 'positivistic fallacy'[12] of equating the *desired* and the *desirable* which 'leads to a confusion between reality and social desirability'.[13] Phenomenological values are central to Hofstede's study, and he views them, along with many social scientists,[14] as criteria affecting how actions are selected and justified, how people and events are evaluated, and how reality is socially constructed. The emphasis upon *desired* values is not, it should be noted, universally accepted, as values are regarded by one source as normative propositions concerning the *desirable*.[15] A problem with Hofstede's study is that it is based upon certain assumptions which many of his critics have difficulty in accepting. The most convincing alternative paradigm is provided by the more recent work of Schwartz.[16] This is not reviewed here, however, as it is covered in some depth elsewhere.[17] In the replication attempted here, Hofstede's assumptions are upheld but some attempt is made to identify where and how they are contentious.

It seems clear, from Hofstede's perspective, that values and culture are interrelated and interdependent as 'values are among the building blocks of culture.'[18] As values are assumed to be the core of culture, then understanding value differences enables an understanding of cultural differences. Culture confers *identity* on a human group at a macro (societal /national) level. Hofstede uses the term 'sub culture' to describe micro-level cultural systems like organizations or ethnic groups. One limitation is that countries have been used as a matter of expediency, as in the original study, as a *proxy* for culture. Sub-cultural differences are not examined by Hofstede or in this article, as this is a completely different level of analysis to cross-national psychology, and termed 'ethnic psychology' by one source.[19] Examinations of sub-cultural differences are important and have been conducted in one study for Chinese-populated regions, including Hong Kong, Taiwan and People's Republic of China samples.[20] These differences suggest that culture is not homogeneous in Chinese societies, and that Hong Kong cannot be regarded as 'representative' of Chinese culture. It should be noted, however, that no claim for Hong Kong being representative is made in this replication and also that the results obtained by this Chinese study are questionable for the two mainland China samples.[21] The submission for this study is that the more substantive differences between Western and Chinese culture than within the latter justifies the comparison between a Western and a Chinese society, as indicators of difference at a broad level of analysis. This is to suggest that a 'compositional view' of national culture is an important foundation for a further 'decompositional' differentiation based on subculture,[22] and a premature pursuit of the latter without an established understanding of the former is in danger of social science failing to see the 'forest' for the 'trees'.

Culture for Hofstede concerns societies as social systems in homeostatic, quasi-equilibrium with societal norms or value systems at the centre interacting with 'ecological' origins and institutional 'consequences'. Hofstede contends that analyses of values at the individual level cannot be equated simultaneously with analyses at the ecological (collective, societal, cultural) level and to do so is an 'ecological fallacy',[23] which confuses two separate and incompatible levels of analysis. This proposition is contentious, and is challenged most frequently by other psychologists concerned that 'the ecological or culture level approach (of Hofstede) does not yield individual level dimensions of values',[24] and it is challenged by another study discovering that, 'in contrast to Hofstede's (1980) findings, the dimensions derived at the two levels in our research appear to be closely related'.[25] It is also suggested by Hofstede that mental programmes are intangible and exist as 'constructs', which are terms we use to define them into existence. This is fraught with problems, as constructs are vulnerable to subjectivity and to the values of their creator and one's own cultural background. Hofstede's study involves the examination of culture at a national level. It is based on the assumption that culture is an appropriate phenomenon at the level of countries or nations. This is contentious as many nations (such as Malaysia for example) are characterized by sub-cultural divisions. The argument in favour of using national culture is that it is a general macro level of analysis enabling general comparisons as a basis for further detailed sub-cultural investigation.

NATIONAL CULTURE

The cultural environment of Hong Kong at a macro level has been delineated by Hofstede within a set of cultural maps of the world,[26] and categorized initially on four dimensions including 'Power Distance', 'Uncertainty Avoidance', 'Individualism–Collectivism' and 'Masculinity–Femininity'.

Power Distance (PDI)

Power Distance informs us about dependence relationships. In countries with large PDI scores, where subordinates feel dependent on their superiors, the result will either be a preference for an autocratic/paternalistic boss or an outright rejection and resentment of the boss, but there is little indifference since the relationship is *morally* based. In contrast, within low scoring PDI countries, there is less of a dependence and more of a *contractual* relationship between subordinates and superiors, resulting in a preference for a consultative rather than autocratic style of leadership. PDI therefore can be defined as 'the extent to which the less powerful members of institutions and organizations within a country expect and accept that power is distributed unequally'.[27] The source of PDI differences in the workplace is, according to Hofstede, in earlier periods of socialization when 'attitudes towards parents, especially fathers, and towards teachers, which are part of our mental programming, are transferred towards bosses.'[28] It is the intention here to explore what changes in PDI have occurred in Hong Kong (and the UK) *to determine whether the key differences identified in Hofstede's original 4-D study still exist.* Hofstede is highly pessimistic about any likelihood of convergence of PDI since nobody ' has offered evidence of a convergence of countries towards smaller power distances since 1972, nor towards smaller *differences* in power distance.'[29] He seems to think it more likely that cultural drift will be simultaneous: 'The cultures shift , but they shift together, so that the differences between them remain intact'.[30]

Individualism–Collectivism (IDV)

This dimension concerns the degree of *dependence of individuals upon the group.* Hofstede provides a definition as:

> Individualism pertains to societies in which the ties between individuals are loose: everyone is expected to look after himself or herself and his or her immediate family. Collectivism as its opposite pertains to societies in which people from birth onwards are integrated into strong, cohesive ingroups, which throughout people's lifetime continue to protect them in exchange for unquestioning loyalty .'[31]

This dimension tends to be negatively correlated with power distance. Hong Kong in the 1980 4-D study was shown to be a large power distant and low individualist (more collective) country, in contrast to the UK which was low power distant but highly individualistic. Both dimensions were correlated with economic development with both countries representing profiles characteristic of developing and developed economies respectively. In the workplace, this dimension fundamentally affects the relationship between the employee and the organization. In highly individualistic societies, this relationship is largely *contractual* and work is mostly organized and controlled with reference to the individual. In contrast, in collectivist societies, the employment relationship is more *morally based,* and the management of groups is salient with personal relationships prevailing over the task, with trust being the essential requirement for successful co-operation. Hofstede maintains that East Asian communities 'seem to have retained considerable collectivism in spite of industrialization',[32] because of the 'influence of the teachings of Confucius',[33] whilst accepting that this dimension is the most likely area of international convergence.

Masculinity–Femininity (MAS)

This dimension concerns the extent to which values are more 'masculine' (assertive, *competitive*, tough, results or performance oriented) in contrast to more 'feminine' (modest, *co-operative*, nurturing, tender, equity oriented). Both Hong Kong and the UK scored as 'moderately masculine' in the original 4-D study,[34] with the UK having a higher MAS score than Hong

Kong. The fundamental consequence for the workplace is that the work ethos in 'masculine' cultures tends towards 'live in order to work ' rather than in 'feminine' cultures where the ethos is more inclined towards 'work in order to live'.[35] This has consequences for how conflicts are resolved (by combat or compromise) and the types of motivation likely to be used (achievement/ goal or welfare/socially oriented), as well as differences in the likely characteristics of 'heroes' (assertive/decisive or intuitive/ consensus seeking). In replicating the original 4-D study, we are looking to see if the similarities that were shown between Hong Kong and the UK still persist today.

Uncertainty Avoidance (UAI)

This dimension concerns 'the extent to which the members of a culture feel threatened by uncertain or unknown futures and situations. This feeling is, amongst other things, expressed through nervous stress and in a need for predictability: a need for written and unwritten rules'.[36] Both Hong Kong and the UK scored relatively low on UAI scores, interpreted, *initially*, as meaning that they both seemed to have a high degree of tolerance of ambiguity and unpredictable situations. This would also suggest a relatively high aversion at the workplace in both countries to 'formal laws and/or informal rules controlling the rights and duties of employers and employees',[37] except where necessary. In other words, there existed a rather pragmatic approach to work. Again, the purpose of this study is to determine if the similarities between Hong Kong and the UK identified in the original 4-D study still persist. It should also be pointed out that UAI (and therefore low UAI scores) may not be significant in Hong Kong, as indicated by the construction of a values survey by Chinese rather than Western minds.

The Chinese Values Survey

Hofstede has more recently added a fifth dimension to his model.[38] This new dimension, derived from the construction of a CVS by The Chinese Culture Connection group is directly relevant to this study, since it concerns 'Confucian Dynamism', which principally relates to the degree of long-termism inherent within a society.[39] This dimension was named in this way since the research indicates that societies influenced by Confucianism (such as China, Hong Kong, Taiwan, Japan and Korea) all share markedly high degrees of long-termism relative to all other countries. Hofstede points out that the CVS resulted in the identification of three out of four of the dimensions identified in his own 4-D study. *None of the CVS factors, however, were correlated with UAI.* This is explained as a fundamental difference between Western and Eastern (particularly Chinese) cultures, which means that Western cultures have a fourth *emic* dimension (UAI) related to different degrees to the search for 'Truth', whereas Chinese societies are more concerned with 'Virtue'. Consequently, the initial interpretation of UAI requires revising, as it is not a relevant dimension for the Chinese. This is not to say that Chinese societies do not face uncertainty and risk, but to make clear that their interpretation and response to the future is intrinsically different from most of the rest of the World. A suggested implication is that this is one of the fundamental reasons for the relative success of countries in the Pacific Rim influenced by Chinese culture. 'By showing the link between Confucian Dynamism and recent economic growth, the CVS research project has demonstrated the strategic advantage of cultures that can practise Virtue without a concern for Truth'.[40]

TABLE 1
CVS DIMENSIONS

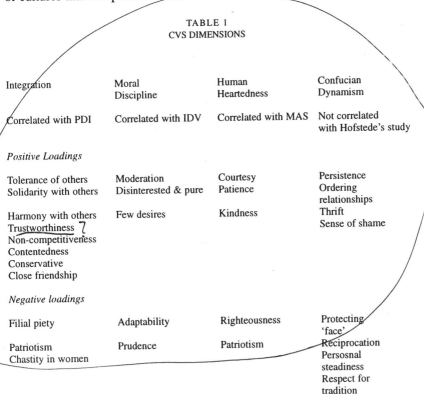

Integration	Moral Discipline	Human Heartedness	Confucian Dynamism
Correlated with PDI	Correlated with IDV	Correlated with MAS	Not correlated with Hofstede's study
Positive Loadings			
Tolerance of others Solidarity with others	Moderation Disinterested & pure	Courtesy Patience	Persistence Ordering relationships
Harmony with others Trustworthiness Non-competitiveness Contentedness Conservative Close friendship	Few desires	Kindness	Thrift Sense of shame
Negative loadings			
Filial piety	Adaptability	Righteousness	Protecting 'face'
Patriotism Chastity in women	Prudence	Patriotism	Reciprocation Persosnal steadiness Respect for tradition

Source: Bond and Hofstede (1989).

Since the CVS research effectively identifies a flaw in the original 4-D survey in that uncertainty avoidance was wrongly presented as an *etic* (cross-culturally comparable), we unfortunately inherit that deficiency in a study replication. It is however possible to compare the results for the three Hofstede and CVS dimensions which do correlate (IDV, PDI and MAS). This disallows reliable comparability for Uncertainty Avoidance, as UAI is not relevant to Chinese respondents. Similarly 'Confucian Dynamism' was not recorded in the original survey and is not examined in the replication. It may also be that 'Confucian Dynamics' may be an inappropriate label for this dimension, since Confucian values are evident in both opposing poles and the term negates the contribution of other influences such as Taoism and Buddhism. Hofstede's adapted term for this dimension of Long Term Orientation (LTO) will also be used in this article. Confucian Dynamism/LTO's suggested significance in terms of comparative advantage is in cultivating a pragmatic synthesis in management where it seems 'What is true or who is right is less important than what works and how the efforts of individuals with different thinking patterns can be co-ordinated towards a common goal'.[41] The elements of the CVS dimensions are shown in Table 1. 'Human-heartedness' on the CVS correlates (negatively) with Masculinity and is characterized by values of kindness, courtesy and social consciousness. 'Integration' correlates (negatively) with PDI and is characterized by the cultivation of trust, tolerance and friendship. 'Moral Discipline' correlates ($r=0.54$) weakly with Collectivism and is characterized by group responsibilities as well as moderate, adaptable and prudent behaviour. This leads us to a discussion of Hong Kong culture in terms of Hofstede's five dimensional model of culture.

HONG KONG CULTURE

Hofstede characterized Hong Kong culture in his 4-D study as similar to Anglo-American culture in that it has weak UAI (or a willingness to accept ambiguity and a low propensity to mitigate uncertainty through a formal, unitary and consensual structure), plus strong MAS (assertive, competitive and materialistic). On the other dimensions, Hong Kong differs sharply from Anglo-American culture by being Collectivist (the moral basis of culture is loyalty to other people in family, clan or organization) and large PDI (hierarchical inequality between dependent subordinates and powerful leading members of society). In addition to having a LTO, they see themselves more as a part or product of the environment than their Western counterpart. Confucian-Taoist-Buddhist societies have a self-concept which is oriented traditionally, and the 'self' is inseperable from its relationships with others. In a Western sense, there is no 'self', as identity is defined through the 'harmony' co-ordinating social mechanisms and ideological systems.[43] It is reflective of collective interdependence and social control based upon 'face', which is a 'social ego' more akin to feminine value systems, despite the prevailing higher MAS scores in these countries. Logically, therefore, MAS values differ between the East and the West since their interaction (in the East) with Collective values and high PDI would seem to modify MAS values to a more benign form than the more interpersonally aggressive, competitive Western equivalent. This is reflected in the CVS findings indicating that the situation in Hong Kong 'suggests "feminine" valuing more than "masculine"',[44] when measured on a scale constructed by Chinese minds. In addition to The Chinese Culture Connection study, supportive, complimentary and parallel models to Hofstede's 4-D model of cross-cultural differences exist as well as critiques and competing models. Here we briefly examine some of the critiques.

CRITIQUES OF HOFSTEDE'S STUDY

It has been suggested that Hofstede's model is probably the most widely cited model in social science. It is certainly cited heavily,[45] but it is also heavily criticized and sometimes maligned, reflecting its effect of polarizing academic discourse on management and culture. Major constraints levelled regularly at Hofstede's study are that the dimensions are a product of the era when the samples were taken, that the IBM sample is restrictive and that a single 'attitude survey' is inadequate for the purpose of identification of *etic* values.[46] In reviewing Hofstede's 4-D study, Triandis is largely complimentary, but has a few reservations.[47] His principal objection is that, in concentrating upon work-related values within IBM, Hofstede limits understanding of cultural differences in depth and extent. Triandis suggests that a fuller coverage of the topic in depth requires the inclusion of other levels of cultural difference, involving perception, cognition and action, as well as the inclusion of further dimensions totalling twenty 'including the ones presented by Hofstede'.[48] Other 'supportive opposition' is provided in two reviews of Hofstede's 4-D study,[49] by Goodstein,[50] and Hunt.[51] The criticisms of Hofstede's methodology in these reviews reflect the most common misconceptions about Hofstede's work, which relate to the appropriacy and size of the samples. Most concern has been expressed about the use of IBM as the vehicle for this study which may cause 'some kind of built-in bias in the original sample, because all individuals are employees of a single multinational',[52] or, on the same point, 'a sample of employees from one multinational organization inevitably raises questions when those results are generalized to entire societies'.[53]

On his sampling methods, Hofstede defends the use of IBM and the narrowness of his samples.[54] He emphasizes that IBM was used to satisfy the principal requirement in cross-cultural surveys for functional equivalence, and points out that the measures focus upon the *differences* between the samples rather than the absolute numbers. The implication is that the differences between these narrow, functionally equivalent samples reflect differences between the populations they represent. Sample sizes do not, therefore, need to be very large as 'The smallest sample obviously determines the reliability of the study. However, if a sample is really homogeneous with regard to the criteria under study, there is very little gain in reliability over an absolute sample size of 50.'[55] This sample size of 50 therefore represents the minimum sample size in any replication, including the replication involving Hong Kong and the UK, which is now described.

HERMES REVISITED

Since the inception of the convergence hypothesis,[56] the polarization of arguments as to whether managerial values are diverging or converging may now be seen as somewhat simplistic, as national culture and business environment as opposing influences can result in convergence or divergence as well as 'crossvergence', an interaction creating unique value systems. A recent study indicates evidence of convergence, divergence and crossvergence between Hong Kong, China and the USA,[57] and another finds that executives from Hong Kong were influenced by a combination of Western and Chinese cultural norms.[58] Hofstede, whilst accepting that cultures may (slowly) shift, maintains that they will shift together and their relative positions will be maintained. This view would seem to anticipate synchronous shifts and to refute the likelihood of convergence, divergence or crossvergence. This study aims therefore to determine the nature and extent of cultural change since Hofstede's original study, by using his VSM in the same organization, surveyed more than twenty years ago.

Hofstede's Advice on Reading Mental Programmes

Researcher effects in the social sciences are a universal phenomenon and 'Social science research is like trying to watch a drama in which one is an actor oneself.'[59] Research is also subject to the influence of the dominant paradigm in the discipline in which the researcher was trained, whether he or she adheres to or challenges that paradigm. Before entering a research exercise involving culture, it is essential to realize and minimize where possible the multiplicity of subjective influences that exist. The principal requirement in comparing national cultures, when using surveys based on samples, is functional equivalence in all aspects other than nationality. This, again, is why IBM was used by Hofstede originally and this logic, therefore, applies to the replication attempted here. By maintaining functional equivalence and focusing upon the relative differences in scores rather than the absolute scores, subjective influences, such as changes that IBM have experienced in the intervening period are controlled. The original study was ambitiously extensive in its coverage of 72 national subsidiaries, using more than 116,000 questionnaires, and dealt mainly with employees' work-related values. The differences between the national subsidiaries were treated as representative of the differences between national cultures. The results, therefore, say more about the *differences* between cultures than the cultures themselves and it is these differences that are emphasized in this replication. The main statistical technique employed by Hofstede was factor analysis, and the results were validated against independent data and other sources. The method of clustering countries has also been independently validated by comparing the results of eight studies since 'it appears that countries/nations can be clustered according to similarities on certain cultural dimensions.'[60]

In order to ensure that the data (collected from individuals) was valid at the national level, mean values and other measures of central tendency which aggregate individual responses were compared by Hofstede. Cautions are given against 'using the country scores obtained from the research for the purpose of stereotyping'. In addition, 'The usefulness of the country scores is not for describing individuals , but for the social systems these individuals are likely to have built.'[61] Valuable notes to those considering replications are provided,[62] in an attempt to avoid sub-standard and ill-advised, ethnocentric replications. The original questionnaire was however an instrument designed by Western researchers, which failed to identify the importance of 'long termism' in the Eastern mind. Consequently, this is an inherited weakness that a replication must recognize and accept. Pitfalls to be avoided include the 'ecological fallacy' involving simultaneous use of individual and collective data, discriminating according to other distinctions such as social class or organization, or using loosely matched samples. Also, the *absolute value* of national scores has no meaning other than to describe national *differences,* and attempting to use them for other purposes is fallacious.

Hofstede's Data Collection and Treatment

Hofstede surveyed IBM twice between 1969 and 1972, producing a large database with answers from more than 116,000 questionnaires from 72 subsidiaries in 66 countries. The questionnaire was also used outside and showed similar country differences in values. Data treatment involved using frequency distributions, correlations, factor analysis across individuals, ANOVA (using country, occupation, sex and age as criteria), and ecological correlations, plus ecological factor analysis to determine the dimensions of culture labelled PDI, UAI, IDV and MAS. In order to be able to use the range of parametric tests, the largely ordinal data was treated as quasi-interval data. The results were conceptually related to other international survey results and country level data published by other authors, leading to the identification of seven variables closely related to the 4-D scores. These were wealth, economic growth, latitude , organization and population size , and growth and density.

Through correlations between HERMES and other data, Hofstede conceptually relates the interactive effects of the four dimensions,[63] and particularly:

- The affect upon organization structures, functioning and reception of theories of the interaction between PDI and UAI;
- The interaction of UAI and MAS is shown to relate to the different dominant motivation pattern within countries.

Hofstede is able to categorize countries into eleven cultural clusters, using a hierarchical cluster analysis.[64] In the resulting 'dendogram', Hong Kong occupies (along with Singapore, India and The Philippines) a separate category from the UK, which inhabits the same cluster as the USA, Australia, Canada, Ireland and New Zealand.

Before examining the concomitants of the cultural dimensions for doing business in Hong Kong or with Hong Kong Chinese companies, it is necessary to examine whether the differences between countries identified by Hofstede are extant after more than twenty years or, if they have changed, whether the evidence suggests this is convergent, divergent or 'crossvergent' change. Hofstede compared his 1969 data with the 1972 data, and showed a combined age and societal change (*Zeitgeist*) effect for PDI and UAI, indicating a decreased desire for PDI and an increase in the component of UAI world-wide during this period.[65] This analysis also indicated increasing Individualism and MAS but little evidence of convergency, leading to a speculation that in the longer term individualism will increase and the PDI norm will decrease as long as national wealth increases, that UAI – or at least its anxiety component – fluctuates over time with a 25–40 year wave length, and that MAS differences among countries will remain large.

This influences the hypotheses to be tested here, which are:

H[1]: *UK and Hong Kong Scores for PDI, IDV and MAS will move in the same direction between the two sample points of 1969-72 and 1993, with IDV rising , PDI falling.* Results demonstrating movement in the same direction support the proposition of *relative* stability in these dimensions. Thus, for example, if PDI for Hong Kong falls and PDI for the UK also falls, this encourages a submission of relative stability.

H[2]: *UK and Hong Kong Scores will move between 1969–72 and 1993 at the same velocity so that the relative difference between them will remain the same.* Results demonstrating stable relative velocity and movement in the same direction would support Hofstede's proposition of synchronous change. Thus if PDI for Hong Kong fell by ten points and PDI for the UK fell by ten points also, then this would support Hofstede's proposition.

Research Design,Collection and Treatment

Senior managers at HERMES in Hong Kong and the UK were contacted in the early part of 1993 and agreed to participate in a replication of Hofstede's 4-D study using the VSM recommended for future cross-cultural survey studies, and as provided by Hofstede in 'Culture's Consequences'.[66] This contains questions which proved most meaningful in ecological differentiation, plus new questions covering issues which the original questionnaires missed.[67] Means were calculated for each variable to compare with previous scores. Little detail of measures of dispersion for the original data , however, survive and this makes a second future survey highly desirable. The scores for the four dimensions of PDI , IDV, UAI and MAS were calculated for both samples, using approximation formulae produced and provided by Hofstede.[68] These scores are shown in Table 2. The results for UAI were calculated but are not included in the hypotheses, as this dimension has been shown through the use of the CVS not to be relevant to Chinese respondents. In order to assess variables within the data, Crosstabs and Chi-squares for each country by all VSM variables were derived.

TABLE 2
SUMMARY OF RESULTS OF 4D STUDY

	Hong Kong		UK	
	1972 (n=88)	1993 (n=139)	1972 (n=6967)	1993 (n=65)
PDI score	68	56	35	16
IDV score *	25	37 (33)	89	87 (92)
MAS score	57	55	66	56
UAI score	29	44	35	31

* 1993 scores controlled for age (unadjusted scores shown in brackets)

Comments on scores

Given that the variability of the original data cannot be fully determined, the interpretation of the data should be treated with caution. The absolute scores are influenced by too many factors to be a reliable indicator of change so attention should focus *solely* upon the relative scores (Table 3). Generally, the changes in relative scores are modest and remarkably similar to each other, confirming Hofstede's prediction that cultural change is a slow process. Indeed, the results show the two countries remaining in the classifications assigned to them in the original study. The differences between the two countries continue to be large, with Hong Kong remaining weak in UAI, large in PDI, Collectivist and moderately Masculine country, just as the UK remains weak in UAI, small in PDI, Individualist and moderately Masculine country. The PDI and MAS scores have moved in the same direction, although not exactly at the same velocity. The UAI scores are moving divergently. However, the UAI scores are not included in the hypothesis as they are less relevant to Chinese respondents.

Further statistical tests on this data is considered inadvisable since the scores represent indices, *not* means, arrived at by using approximation formulae,[69] which control the occupation effect. We are restricted to examining the relative scores and interpreting their meaning without further statistical analysis. This is acceptable, as we are simply solely focusing upon the relative *differences* in indices between two sample points.

PDI

As predicted by Hofstede, the PDI norm has fallen as both countries have experienced economic growth. Absolute scores are lower in the 1993 replication than in the original study, but, because the UK PDI score has fallen more sharply, the relative difference between scores is greater in 1993 than it was in the original study. This is indicative of 'crossvergence'. A higher level of growth in Hong Kong does not explain the different velocities, since this would have resulted in the Hong Kong PDI falling more sharply.

IDV

A factor which needs to be accounted for here is the effect of age differences between samples, as older respondents are likely to score higher on average IDV scores on the VSM.[70] For the results to be reliable, the samples need to be matched on age, gender, education and job type.[71] No further detail of demographic variables is needed except to confirm matched equivalence in the samples. As the two samples are matched on all required variables other than age (see Table 3), adjustment was made to control for age,[72] as it affects IDV using an appropriate regression equation. The Hong Kong score is higher in 1993 than in the original study. A sharp rise in the Hong Kong score reduces the difference between the two countries (although the remaining difference is still substantial), and the apparent difference in velocity may be attributable to a higher economic growth rate in Hong Kong than in the UK over the past two decades. The UK score which is controlled for age is actually marginally lower in 1993. This is contrary to Hofstede's predictions and the outcome seems indicative of convergence.

TABLE 3
DIFFERENCES IN SCORES BETWEEN UK AND HONG KONG

	1972	1993
PDI score	-33	-40
IDV score	64	50
MAS score	9	1
UAI score	6	-13

MAS

Both scores are lower in 1993 than in the original study. As both countries have experienced economic growth during this period, this is consonant with Hofstede's predictions. The difference between the UK and Hong Kong is even smaller than it was in 1972 since the UK score has dropped more sharply than Hong Kong. This is indicative of convergence. The hypothesis H1 is proven for PDI and MAS, as the scores indicate movement in the same direction for both countries. This hypothesis does not hold for IDV, it has not increased for the UK when the IDV score is controlled for age differences between the samples.

The hypothesis H^2 is not proven, as the velocity of change is not identical, *although similar* for both countries in IDV, PDI and MAS. In hindsight, the second hypothesis may have been too rigid as influences such as widely different rates of economic growth between the two sample countries and the effect of age differences in the two samples upon the IDV score mean that matched velocity was highly unlikely. A better solution may have been to hypothesize upon relative rather than absolute velocity. Nevertheless, and despite these factors, the fact that for IDV, PDI and MAS the differences between the countries has not changed by more than 14 points is an indication of relatively equivalent velocity of movement. Both hypotheses, in effect, cannot be proven but the relationships between variables do appear to behave generally in accordance with Hofstede's expectations.

FIGURE 1
POSITION OF UK AND HK ON PDI AND IDV INDICES 1972 AND 1993
(PRIVATE)

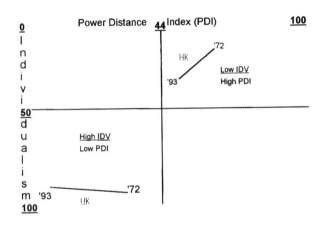

A Chi-square test was conducted to determine the significance of each of each VSM question as ecological (between country) indicators. If a question proves significant it is a variable sensitive in differentiating cultural values. Table 4 largely vindicates VSM variables as suitable ecological indicators. All the principal indicators except Q13 and Q27 from the original study prove significant here also.[73] From the new questions there is an indication that Q12, Q15 and Q18 may warrant inclusion as principal indicators in future studies.

SUMMARY AND CONCLUSIONS

This article examines Hofstede's 4-D model of culture as international differences in work-related values. The role of culture from Hofstede's perspective is reviewed and it is made clear that this is not the only perspective, as it is based upon certain assumptions which are not

TABLE 4
CHI-SQUARE (COUNTRY BY ALL VSM VARIABLES)

Question	Type	Summary of Question	Chi-sq Value	Significance Level
Q1	Original (A18)	Importance of job with sufficient personal/family time	7.007	0.03(a)
Q2	Original (A5)	Importance of challenging tasks or sense of accomplishment	9.927	0.006(b)
Q3	New question	Importance of little tension & stress	16.893	0.002(b)
Q4	Original (A12)	Importance of good physical working conditions	18.271	0.003(b)
Q5	Original (A16)	Importance of good relationship with superior	8.079	0.017(b)
Q6	Original (A14)	Importance of job security	22.603	0.0001(c)
Q7	Original (A13)	Importance of job with considerable scope to adopt own approach	4.561	Not significant
Q8	Original (A8)	Importance of working with people who cooperate well	20.235	0.00004(c)
Q9	New question	Importance of being consulted by direct superior	3.273	Not significant
Q10	Original (C3)	Importance of making contribution to success of organization	3.345	Not significant
Q11	Original (A7)	Importance of opportunity for higher earnings	15.548	0.0004(c)
Q12	New question	Importance of serving country	32.459	0.0000(c)
Q13	Original (A6)	Importance of living in desirable area	1.601	Not significant
Q14	Original (A15)	Importance of chance for advancement	10.381	0.005(b)
Q15	New question	Importance of variety and adventure	14.921	0.005(b)
Q16	New question	Importance of prestigious, successful organization	3.391	Not significant
Q17	New question	Importance of chance to help others	6.259	Not significant
Q18	New question	Importance of well-defined role	31.064	0.0000(c)
Q19	Original (A54)	Prefer autocratic, communicative, consulting, democratic manager	10.774	0.013(b)
Q20	Original (A56)	If current manager any of above	7.089	Not significant
Q21	Original (A37)	How often feel nervous or tense	15.516	0.0001(c)
Q22	Original (B6)	Degree of (dis)agreement on inviolability of company rules	20.051	0.0001(c)
Q23	New question	Degree of (dis)agreement on trustworthiness of most people	1.831	Not significant
Q24	Original (C13)	Degree of (dis)agreement that a few employees workshy	43.484	0.0000(c)
Q25	Original (C17)	Degree of (dis)agreement that large better than small employer	12.979	0.004(c)
Q26	Original (B46)	Frequency subordinates frightened to disagree with superior	48.926	0.0000(c)
Q27	Original (A43)	Expected time working for organization	4.222	Not significant
Q28	Original (A1)	Sex	2.227	Not significant
Q29	Original (A57)	Age	27.012	0.00002(c)
Q30	Original (A56)	Formal education	1.454	Not significant
Q31	Job Type		3.981	Not significant

Notes: Significant at (a) 0.05 level; (b) 0.01 level; (c) 0.005 level. Reference to original questions in the second column refer to those used in Hofstede's original study.

universally accepted. Hofstede's 'compositional' model seeks to identify 'etics' at a macro (national) level of analysis and the constructs that emerge reflect that fact. The subsequent identification of a fifth dimension shows a weakness in the original model since the identification of a Chinese 'emic' means that the original study had a Western bias and, since UAI is not relevant to the Chinese, UAI does not qualify as an 'etic' dimension like PDI, IDV and MAS. The brief review of some of the critiques of Hofstede's study reveals some common misconceptions. The greatest of these is the view that Hofstede's model measures 'culture'. In fact, Hofstede's constructs enable the measurement of 'emic' cultural *differences*, which is subtly but importantly distinct from 'measuring culture'. In my view, much of the criticism of Hofstede is unreasonable, as it attributes aspects to the model that Hofstede has never claimed or in some cases has disclaimed. Some of the criticism seems to be attributable to the seminal and 'high profile' status of the model, which encourages greater attention and some of it is based on a misunderstanding of the detail. The model is, however, not perfect, but no model can be as all models are gross oversimplifications of a reality too complex for the human mind to comprehend. In this sense, Hofstede's model is a foundation that social scientists must add to and reformulate in the light of new knowledge.

In conclusion, the results of this replication show that Hofstede's dimensions do not move synchronously. However, in keeping with Hofstede's expectations , the dimensions appear to change slowly and the substantive differences between Hong Kong and the UK remain unchanged. The results do not confirm Hofstede's specific propositions as to how these dimensions would change but at a broad level Hofstede's model is validated as the differences between the cultures remain relatively stable. This is made more significant by the fact that this stability has been identified in this replication using the same vehicle as in Hofstede's original study. The main consequence is to reaffirm support for the theory that management is culture-bound rather than culture-free and to question whether Western management theories can apply in Hong Kong or in the Asia Pacific generally. The submission is that a re-examination of this question is overdue and the hope is that it may re-appear on the agenda for discussion amongst social scientists interested in developments in the Asia Pacific.

ACKNOWLEDGMENTS

The author would like to thank Geert Hofstede for his advice and comments on successive drafts of this article. Thanks are also offered to Peter Milligan of King's College, London and John Whitman of the University of Hong Kong for statistical advice.

NOTES

1. R.S. Bhaget and S.J. McQuaid, 'Role of Subjective Culture in Organisations : A Review and Directions for Future Research', *Journal of Applied Psychology Monograph*, Vol.67, No.5 (October 1982).
2. G. Hofstede, *Culture's Consequences* (1984) (abridged), p.15.

3. Ajiferuke and Boddewyn, 'Culture' and Other Explanatory Variables in Comparative Management Studies', *Academy of Management Journal*, Vol. 13 (1970), 153–63; N. Adler, 'A Typology of Management Studies Involving Culture', *Journal of International Business Studies* (Fall 1983), pp.29–47.
4. H.C. Triandis, 'Review of Culture's Consequences : International Differences in Work-Related Values', *Human Organisation*. Vol.41, No.1 (Spring 1982).
5. Ronen and Shenkar, 'Clustering Countries on Attitudinal Dimensions : A Review and Synthesis', *Academy of Management Review*, Vol.10, No.3 (1985), pp.435–54.
6. N. Bosland, 'An Evaluation of Replication Studies Using The Values Survey Module', Working Paper 85–2, IRIC, Rijksuniversiteit Limburg, The Netherlands (1985), p.16.
7. Triandis,'Review of Culture's Consequences', p.86.
8. G. Hofstede, *Culture and Organisations* (1991), p.5.
9. Hofstede, *Culture's Consequences,* 1984, p.21.
10. Ibid. p.18.
11. Ibid.
12. Ibid. p.19.
13. Ibid.
14. S.H. Schwartz, 'Universals in the Content and Structure of values : Theoretical Advances and Empirical Tests in 20 Countries', *Advances in Experimental Social Psychology* (1992), p.1.
15. P.E. Jacob and K.K. Flink, 'Values and their Function in Decision Making', *American Behavioural Scientist* (May 1962), p.22.
16. S.H. Schwartz, 'Beyond Individualism/Collectivism; New Cultural Dimensions of Values' in Kim et.al. (eds.), *Individualism and Collectivism; Theory , Method, and Applications* (1994), pp.85–119.
17. S. Lowe and C. Oswick, 'Culture : The Invisible Filters' in S. Gatley, R. Lessem and Y. Altman (eds.), in *Corporate Management: A Transcultural Odyssey*, McGraw-Hill (1996).
18. Hofstede, 'Culture's Consequences', p.21.
19. J.W. Berry *et al.*, *Cross-Cultural Psychology: Research and Applications* (1992), p.2
20. P.Y. Huo and D. Randall, 'Exploring Subcultural Differences in Hofstede's Value Survey : The Case of The Chinese', *Asia Pacific Journal of Management*,Vol.8, No.2 (1991), pp.159–173.
21. N. Bosland, 'An Evaluation', p.16.
22. P.Y. Huo and D.M. Randall, 'Exploring Subcultural Differences', p.160.
23. Hofstede, 'Culture's Consequences', p.24.
24. M.H. Bond, 'Finding Universal Dimensions of Individual Variation in Multicultural Studies of Values: the Rokeach and Chinese Value Surveys', *Journal of Personality and Social Psychology*, Vol.55, No.6 (1988), pp.1009–15.
25. S.H. Schwartz, 'Beyond Individualism/Collectivism', p.2.
26. G. Hofstede, 'Culture's Consequences'.
27. Ibid., p.27.
28. Ibid., p.35.
29. Ibid., p.47.
30. Ibid., p.77.
31. Ibid., p.51.
32. Ibid., p.74.
33. Ibid., p.77.
34. Ibid., p.85.
35. Ibid., p.93.
36. Ibid., p.113.
37. Ibid., p.120.
38. Ibid.
39. M.H. Bond, 'Chinese Values and the Search for Culture-Free Dimensions of Culture: The Chinese Culture Connection', *Journal of Cross-Cultural Psychology*, Vol.18 No.2 (1987), pp.143–64.
40. G. Hofstede, 'Culture's Consequences', p.172.
41. Ibid., p.172.
42. M.H. Bond and G. Hofstede, 'The Cash Value of Confucian Values', *Human Systems Management*, Vol.8 (1989), p.196.
43. R.I. Westwood, *Organisation Behaviour : Southeast Asian Perspectives* (1992), p.50.
44. Bond, 'Chinese Values', p.152.

45. M. Sondergaard, 'Research Note : Hofstede's Consequences : A Study of Reviews,Citations and Replications', *Organisation Studies*, Vol.15 (1994), p.448.
46. Ibid., p.449.
47. Triandis, 'Review of Culture's Consequences'.
48. Ibid., p.88.
49. G. Hofstede, 'Do American Theories Apply Abroad ? A Reply to Goodstein and Hunt', *Organisational Dynamics*, Summer (1981), p.63.
50. L.D. Goodstein, 'American Business Values and Cultural Imperialism', *Organisational Dynamics*, Summer (1981), pp.49–54.
51. J.W. Hunt, 'Applying American Behavioural Science : Some Cross-Cultural Problems', *Organisational Dynamics*, Summer (1981), pp.55–62.
52. Goodstein, 'American Business Values', p.51.
53. J.W.Hunt, 'Applying American Behavioural Science', p.55.
54. Hofstede, 'Do American Theories Apply Abroad', p.64.
55. Ibid. p.65.
56. C. Kerr *et al., Industrialism and Industrial Man* (1960).
57. D. Ralston *et al*, 'Differences in Managerial Values: A Study of U.S and PRC Managers ', *Journal of International Business Studies* (1993).
58. D. Tse *et al.*, 'Does Culture Matter? A Cross-Cultural Study of Executives' Choice, Decisiveness, and Risk Adjustment in International Marketing', *Journal of Marketing*, Vol.52 (1988), pp.81–95.
59. Hofstede, 'Culture and Organisations', p.248.
60. S. Ronen and O.Shenkar, 'Clustering Countries on Attitudinal Dimensions : A Review and Synthesis', *Academy of Management Review*, Vol.10, No.3 (1985), pp.435–54.
61. Hofstede, 'Culture and Organisations (1991), p.253.
62. Ibid. p.254.
63. Hofstede, 'Culture's Consequences'.
64. Ibid. p.229.
65. Hofstede used the VSM question 19, 'preferred manager', for estimating Power Distance and on- the -job stress, and the 'nervous or tense' question, number 21, for estimating Uncertainty Avoidance, as these were shown to be more reliable indicators over time.
66. Hofstede, 'Culture's Consequences', Appendix 1.
67. Ibid.
68. G. Hofstede, *Scoring Guide for VSM* (1982).
69. Ibid.
70. Huo and Randall, 'exploring Subcultural Differences', p.171.
71. Ibid., p.160.
72. Ibid., p.171.
73. Hofstede, 'Culture's Consequences', Appendix 1.

Culture's Consequences for Management in Hong Kong

SID LOWE

INTRODUCTION

In a recent review of Hofstede's comparative study of business practice and national cultures,[1] 61 works replicating his methods[2] are identified, and the critical four differences in the cultural dimension are 'largely confirmed'.[3] The only replication of Hofstede's study within IBM (his original sample vehicle, and given the pseudonym 'Hermes') has largely validated the original model some 20 years later.[4] These results seem to validate the valuable contribution of Hofstede's work, although his model contains the limitations of all models; the simplification of reality into an understandable form cannot do justice to its complexity.[5] In this article, the main consequences of Hofstede's work for Hong Kong are reviewed. His proposition that culture, and particularly social values, influence economic activity and management, which is consequently 'culture-bound', is restated and supported by more recent studies.

APPROACHES TO STUDYING 'CULTURE'

'Emic' or 'Etic': Culture-free or Culture-bound?

In comparing cultures, Hofstede is assuming that sufficient similarities exist to enable comparison. The dispute between those studying culture who seek to examine similarities and those examining differences, between the comparable and the unique, between those employing 'nomothetic/etic' to 'idiographic/emic' methods, is a long standing one.[6] Hofstede's study subjectively presupposes a more 'etic' point of departure and seeks to identify generalizable laws which are at the same time least sensitive to the uniqueness of each culture.[7] Hofstede proposes that a focus upon similarities and differences combined with a distinction between different (micro and macro) levels of analysis provides a useful typology of research strategies. This is shown in Table 1. Hofstede's justification for choosing a 'Cell 4' approach is to focus on cultural differences between societies to refute the culture-free hypothesis. This proposes that different contingency variables rather than 'culture' explain differences between organizations in different societies. An extreme form of this advocacy of the universality of laws is the proposition of an expected global convergence in organizational

Sid Lowe, King's College, London

characteristics due to the universally homogenizing effect of the diffusion of technology.[8]

TABLE 1
RESEARCH STRATEGIES FOR COMPARATIVE MULTISOCIETY STUDIES

	Focus on similarities between societies	Focus on differences between societies
Concerned with micro-level variables within societies	1.Prove universality of micro-level laws	2. Illustrate uniqueness of each society
Concerned with macro-level variables within societies	3. Determine types or subsets of societies	4. Determine dimensions of societies and macro-level laws

Source: Hofstede (1984).

Hofstede's study, in identifying cultural differences between societies and in recognizing 'cultural relativism' in work-related values, supports the proposition that work, management, and organizations are 'culture-bound' rather than 'culture-free'. The results of the replications of his famous 4-D study,[9] which show stability in cultural differences, serve to further support the culture-bound hypothesis. Culture is assumed to act as an intervening variable, in the form of 'societal norms' as value systems, filtering an interpretation of the environment which accumulates to the development and pattern maintenance of institutions in society.[10] These institutions (including the category of organizations) in turn reinforce the societal norms and environmental conditions that created them, a 'loop' which enables cultural patterns to remain in stable equilibrium for long periods. Thus, institutions, in this view, are both a 'consequence' of culture and an instrument in its formulation and reformulation. A similar conceptual framework supporting the role of culture as a 'filter' is provided by another source.[11] In this framework, culture acts as a 'process variable' intervening between the environments (at the population level) and psychological/ behavioural outcomes (at the individual level). There are clear similarities between Hofstede's conception of culture and this framework. A main area of consensus is in the relationship between values and behaviour. Hofstede guards against the 'idealistic assumption'[12] that value change has to precede behaviour since behaviour is situationally contingent. This is further supported elsewhere,[13] and suggests a need to recognize the important situational or 'contextual' dimension in studying management at work. In other words, culture is important enough to be included as an influence but cultural determinism is a danger to be avoided.

Consequently, it is dangerous to regard the concept of culture as deterministic in explaining the economic success of Hong Kong. Therefore, 'the Overseas Chinese have an apparent distinct economic culture, that is describable, and the outline of its determinants can be drawn. It is still necessary to place it in a larger framework of explanation if the question of macro-economic performance is to be considered', and 'it is necessary to reassert that (culture) is not seen as the dominant cause of economic success, obliterating or ignoring other factors like economic policy. Culture is one of several key features, deserving a respectable place in any account'.[14] This framework has several characteristics that assist in enabling an improved understanding of culture and its complex role. Culture is shown as a 'process variable' and an intervening filtering system between contingent macro-level variables or 'situational' factors in the environment and individual level psychological and behavioural responses. The processing role of culture is interdependent with biological or genetic factors. As a result culture as 'nurture' and genetics as 'nature' jointly act as a filtering system of combined learned and inherited mental programmes. Also, it is clear that the cultural/genetic filtering system does not affect all influences from the environment, since some influences from the ecology have direct impact upon the individual, just as acculturation influences directly from the socio-political environment (See Berry et al., 1992, p.12). For instance, the influence of Western culture in Hong Kong has a direct acculturation influence upon the individual, making it very difficult to distinguish what might be causing behaviour or cognition, or what the relative importance of indigenous compared to 'imported' culture is. These complexities mean that any model of culture can only partly capture what is happening in a society. The process we have embarked upon is to look to improve our models and our understanding whilst realizing that perfection is impossible.

Cultural Relativism, Capitalist Development and Management

In accepting the influence of culture and adopting a position of cultural relativism, it can be argued that the influence of social values on development is a suitable foundation for the discourse on different forms of capitalist development.[15] Research into examining the extent of the influence of culture is problematic as the collective (cultural) and individual (psychological/behavioural/relational) aspects of social interaction require simultaneous examination yet do not lend themselves to the same kinds of analysis. This dilemma has been identified as Nadel's Paradox[16] and the consequence has been for social scientists to focus on one aspect of the duality, with 'culture free' relational models seeming more fruitful,[17] although somewhat impoverished by the bypassing or denigration of normative aspects of roles and the consequent privilege afforded to rational-actor models from the resulting intellectual void. The neo-institutionalist solution to Nadel's paradox is in its infancy but its identification is an opportunity to extend structural analysis into the cultural realm, involving the 'practical-actor' conceptions of actions and the structuration[18] of relational networks[19] by concentrating more upon the cognitive influences of culture, rather than the evaluative influences emphasized by Hofstede and the majority of models within social psychology.

UNDERSTANDING CULTURAL DIVERSITY

The Seven Cultures of Capitalism

In collaboration with Hampden-Turner, Trompenaars applies cultural dimensions developed in an earlier work[20] to six Western industrial countries plus Japan.[21] In this text, the dimension 'neutral versus emotional' is replaced with an alternative dimension 'equality versus hierarchy', which appears to closely resemble Hofstede's Power Distance (PDI). Not surprisingly, the major dichotomy is shown between Anglo-Saxon and Japanese culture with France, Germany, Holland and Sweden adopting varying positions between them. The message of Hampden-Turner and Trompenaars is to submit that it is necessary to recognize and reconcile differences and attempt to synthesize the advantages inherent in all cultures. It is a re-iteration of the view that there in no 'one best way' of managing and no objective truth in how best to generate economic development and wealth. The mechanistic metaphors attributed to organizations and markets is largely a product of Anglo-Saxon culture which cultivates a tendency towards 'scientific management'. Cultures which most tenaciously hold to this mechanistic model are the poorest performers even by their own 'objective' measurements, except perhaps in commodity markets where quality and value-added are less important. In support of this, it has been stated:

> Clearly, the recognition of 'culture relativism' in people's social and work values is a lever, if not a corrective, to the hegemonic yet optimistic assumption implied often by the 'scientific managers' (or even subscribers to the Weberian 'bureaucratic' ideal type or the enlightened Human Relations School) that there exists a universal or 'monolithic' prescription for the management of human and work organizations.[22]

Another general misconception is that East Asian cultures as a homogenous Confucian entity are best represented by Japan. Confucianism may be a significant dimension in the region but recent studies indicate 'emics' and 'etics' between these countries[23] and within them.[24] As a result, Confucianism can be expected to have differential influence in the region, as it will interrelate with different cultural configurations in each society in different ways. Hofstede's results also differentiate between East Asian societies on his 'etic' dimensions, with, for example, Japan showing a unique cultural profile which predicts differences in structure and behaviour with its immediate neighbours. In a replication of Hofstede's 4-D study undertaken within IBM,[25] the UK is compared to Hong Kong and, although the scores between the two sample points do not change synchronously, the differences between the two countries remains substantial, reflecting the typically large differences between the West and the East. Further research involving IBM subsidiaries in other Western and East Asian societies would be needed to more comprehensively validate Hofstede's 1980 study.

Chinese Culture and Chinese Management

The differences in cultural characteristics and particularly in values, identified by Hofstede, suggest that different world views are likely to engender different approaches to work, organization and management. One influence of culture upon organizations suggested by Hofstede is through structure. Hofstede maintains that structure has cultural antecedents and suggests that culture will influence 'implicit models' of organizations which will influence the norm of preferred configuration of structure. The implicit model for Hong Kong organizations is the 'family model' and the corresponding preferred configuration is the 'simple structure', which is characterized by a preference for direct supervision by the 'strategic apex'. This, for most, reflects the relatively high PDI and weak Uncertainty Avoidance (UAI) (or high Confucian Dynamism) of Chinese culture, which has the effect of promoting centralized concentration of authority/power and the weak structuring of activities. This hypothesis has been partly validated by a recent study which confirmed the association of PDI and authority but failed to confirm an association of UAI and structural differentiation.[26]

TABLE 2
CULTURE AND MODELS OF ORGANIZATION

Dominant Cultural Influence	Reason for Action	Response/Model of Organization	Organizing Principles
Individualism	'In my interest'	Private ownership/market	Incentives/prices
High uncertainty avoidance	'Follow rules'	External authority/ bureaucracy	Rules/authority/ hierarchy
Collectivism	'The way we do things'	Collective cooperation/ self-restraint/community	Norms/values/ affiliation/trust/ networks

Source: Adapted from Colebach and Larmour (1993), p.17.

Support for the proposition that implicit models of organizations and organizational structure have cultural antecedents comes from an eclectic array of social scientists from various disciplines. It has been suggested that dominant models of organizations correspond to reasons for action and concomitant responses.[27] The suggestion here is that these reasons and responses are culture-bound. This is represented in Table 2. The submission here is that, whereas PDI and UAI are the likely principal influences upon organizational structure, Individualism and Collectivism is likely to be additionally instrumental in the ideological and political processes that promote models of organization within cultures. A similar approach is adopted by Schneider,[28] who suggests that strategic issues within organizations are formulated in a national cultural context. Strategic issues involving 'relationships with the environment' involve questions of 'coping with uncertainty' (UAI) and assessing 'truth' (LTO/Confucian Dynamism).

Other issues encompass 'internal relationships' involving questions of 'power and status' (PDI), Individualism (IDV) and 'social orientation' (Collectivism). Corporate culture may influence the beliefs and values affecting the behaviour of individuals but the relationship between the variables is not straightforward, as it is dependent upon the broader (ethnic/national) cultural environment.[29]

In developing a theory of 'community', Taylor[30] has developed a model which identifies the essential elements as common beliefs and values, direct and diffuse relationships, and reciprocity.[31] This model is supported by others,[32] but the term 'network' is often preferred to community, in order to describe the alternative to exchange based on self-interest or hierarchy.

Williamson's[33] theory of 'markets' and 'hierarchies' clearly identifies two of the models in Table 3. Ouchi[34] adds a third as 'clans' to rectify the deficiency in Williamson's model. Whatever the terms used it is clear that the 'network' model is more appropriate to Overseas Chinese (OC) economies such as Hong Kong, Taiwan and Singapore. This is not to say that networks do not exist elsewhere, but to suggest that unlike elsewhere the network 'structure' is the modal form in OC economies with 'markets' and 'hierarchies' comparatively less predominant than in modern *Gesellschaft* societies.[35] The characteristic pattern of networks in OC economies is a high degree of family-based owner management with emerging business groups tied through personal relations and networks of interlocking directorships.[36]

TABLE 3
TYPOLOGY OF MODELS AND STRUCTURES OF ORGANIZATIONS

MODEL CONCOMITANTS

Stevens/Hofstede 'implicit model'	Village Market	Well-oiled Machine	Pyramid of People	Family
Hofstede 'preferred configurations of organizational structure'	Market, Bureaucracy or Adhocracy	Workflow or Professional Bureaucracy	Full Bureaucracy	Simple or Personnel Bureaucracy
Colebatch and Larmour	Market	Bureaucracy	Bureaucracy	Community
Williamson/ Ouchi	Market	Bureaucracy	Clan	Clan
Jarillo/ Thompson *et al.*	Market	Bureaucracy	Clan	Network
Boisot	Market	Bureaucracy	Clan	Fief
Douglas	Type A	Type B	Type C	Type D
Handy	Athena or Dionysus	Apollo	Apollo	Zeus

Two anthropological typologies further support the idea that structure and models of organizations are culture-bound. Boisot[37] posits a framework for 'Culture Space' based upon two variables of Power (or PDI) and Behaviour ('uncodified'/personalistic/collectivist, or 'codified'/ universal/individualistic). The concomitants are four paradigms of social co-ordination: Fiefs, Clans, Bureaucracies and Markets. Douglas's Grid/Group theory[38] is another typology for comparing cultures and associated social institutions, proposing that an individual's values, perceptions and behaviour are shaped and controlled within the domains of 'group commitment' and 'grid control'. The Group dimension resembles Hofstede's Individualism–Collectivism, in representing the focus of society upon the individual or group. Strong group cultures are highly interactive and collectively co-operative, whereas in weak group cultures the individual is less dependent upon groups. The Grid dimension resembles Hofstede's PDI, in distinguishing how status and authority are construed. In strong grid cultures, roles, status and authority are determined by ascriptive social classifications such as age, whereas in weak grid cultures roles are assigned more according to ability and achievement criteria.

Four archetypes result from the combination of these two dimensions providing four scenarios of social life:

- Type A: weak group/weak grid
- Type B: weak group/strong grid
- Type C: strong group/strong grid
- Type D: strong group/weak grid.

Each cosmology or construction of reality stems from the nature of relationships and is thus socially constructed within everyday interaction. Hong Kong would be classed as Type C, whereas the UK would be Type A. The consequences for organizations of this model are also consonant with Hofstede's ideas on culture's consequences for implicit models for organizations and organizational design, although Hofstede considers that a combination of UAI (rather than IDV) and PDI or 'authority' is the critical influence.

Hofstede theorizes that four main implicit models of organizations result from differences in UAI and PDI. In low UAI/low PDI countries like the UK, the implicit model is a 'village market', whereas in low UAI/high PDI countries like Hong Kong, the implicit model is the 'extended family'. These correspond, according to Hofstede, to Williamson's concept of 'market' organizations and Ouchi's concept of 'clans',[39] and significantly, they correspond to Douglas' formulation of organizational structures for different grid/group cultures[40] and to Boisot's 'Culture Space' framework for paradigms of social co-ordination. The consistencies between these models is, in my view, remarkable. Table 1 summarizes the apparent similarities between these models. The outcome provides powerful support for Hofstede's model suggesting that implicit models and modal structures of organizations are culture-bound.

The Eighth Culture of Capitalism : Theory C

A consequence of a persistently uniquely different cultural environment in Hong Kong from most Western countries, as well as, to some extent, Japan,[41] is a rather different type of economic activity. The linkages between societal values and economic performance within OC communities have been investigated in some depth by Redding.[42] In his work, he shows the central importance of values and particularly those associated with familism in partially explaining the source of recent economic success amongst the OC. He also emphasizes the importance of manager-owners who created 'recipes' or cultures in the form of family businesses, which are cultural artifacts peculiarly well suited to the socio-cultural environment and particularly well placed to exploit opportunities in their economic environment. In demonstrating the dominance of family-based businesses in Hong Kong, Redding provides empirical support for Hofstede's model of culturally-influenced organizations which predicts a 'simple structure' for modal organizations in High PDI/Low UAI societies. He describes a distinctive and coherent form of capitalist development largely through investigating the values of founder-leaders who 'together constitute a spirit of Chinese Capitalism'.[43]

The rationale of the success of the OC centres on the concept of an 'economic culture',[44] which describes connections between socio-cultural values and economic behaviour conducive to development. Taoist, Buddhist and Confucian (or, more appropriately, neo-Confucian) ideals and especially familism are one essential source of socio-cultural values which, through the vehicle of the Chinese family business, enable successful economic behaviour.

It should be said that the significance attributed to the role of culture is not shared by all. Some of the now-dominant institutionalist accounts of East Asian business[45] afford a grudging peripheral role to culture in the structural reformulation of institutions during modernization. The transaction cost theories of Williamson[46] explain business structures in terms of cost efficiencies and view networks, the dominant structure in East Asian economies, as hybrids to the 'normal' alternative structures of markets or hierarchies. The differences between the 'culturist' and other approaches is attributable in part to the failure, thus far, to resolve Nadel's paradox. A solution is not proposed here but the submission of this article is that the 'culturist' position is the denigrated 'non-rational' or 'bounded rationality' alternative to the privileged and dominant theories which reflect the rationalist obsessions inherent in the scientific paradigm. As such, the proposition is that a promotion or liberation of the denigrated cultural approach and a cultural deconstruction of the dominant paradigm is prescient. The objective here would be to enrich and rebalance the institutionalist approach rather than destabilize it.

MANAGEMENT CONSEQUENCES

How different is management in Hong Kong? Hofstede maintains that adoption of a culturally relativist stance requires examination of management theories for their relevance outside the national cultures of the authors of the theories. A main objective for future research should be to enable development of indigenous management theory, and to examine why the family-based culture inherent in local Hong Kong organizations has, on the whole, enabled them to prosper particularly well in increasingly chaotic environments. One proposition for future investigation is that the success of Hong Kong firms is due in large part to their adoption of 'cultural filters' which enable them to 'develop an attitude of receptivity and high adaptability to changing conditions'.[47] They seem to have achieved this adaptability despite (or even because of) shortages of Western business skills and techniques in marketing, human resources and other areas.

Hong Kong Chinese firms are in comparison to Western organizations more cohesive, family-based, collective and holistic. Westwood characterizes their structural elements as lower in complexity and formalization, but higher in degree of centralization than their Western and Japanese counterparts,[48] and cites recent Hong Kong studies[49] to support these propositions. Relationships were critically important in 'relationship-centred' Chinese organizations[50] and are founded on a belief in tradition and moral debt amongst people who 'instinctively avoid conflict of loyalties'.[51] Another result of this are distinctive co-operative 'industrial recipes'[52] or wider cultural reference groups. For instance, industries seem dominated by networks which enable formations of flexible temporary 'organizations' in some industries which exploit specific contracts and disband to seek new opportunities on completion. Both networks and constituent organizations are dominated by family-based hierarchies similar to the patron–client hierarchies from the recent rural past. The essence of these traditional structures is to attempt to integrate the interests of both patrons and clients in a trust-based system of mutually beneficial support in what may be described as a 'moral economy',[53] which is self-perpetuated in a virtuous circle by successful growth and controlled through mutual obligation and trust rather than by the rule of law and legal institutions.[54] As a result, the successful cultivation of both networks inside the organization and within the industry is a pre-requisite of success requiring skills at fostering trust, mutual loyalty and balancing autocratic power with paternalistic responsibility. Hong Kong organization as such are consequently relatively 'weak', as the strength, flexibility and durability of Hong Kong business is within the 'recipes' of networks rather than organizations.[55] This means, in research terms, according to Chen and Hamilton, that it is desirable to concentrate research attention on the networks rather than on individual organizations, or in other terms on the linkages between organizations.[56]

This has consequences for marketing and marketing research in Hong Kong, which is a relationship/particularist rather than contractual/

transactional culture. Western marketing theory has been dominated by a 'transactional' view rooted in the American culture which prefers 'markets' to 'hierarchies'. Evidence is emerging as to the fundamental importance of trust in 'Guanxi-qiye' relationships within OC business networks,[57] supporting the proposition that marketing issues cannot be wholly understood by reference to Western models,[58] and implying a research agenda reflecting the 'realities' as understood by 'practical actor' Chinese marketers themselves. Social and cultural values reflecting Confucian ideas and other influences are, consequently, at the core of understanding the OC model of capitalist development. Much work is needed in this area, particularly in the processes of establishing and maintaining 'trust', because, although it is clear that trust as exchange of promises[59] is a critical element in successful 'relationship marketing', its role is still not fully understood.

Hofstede's Consequences for Hong Kong : Do Western Theories Apply?

Hofstede's work adds considerable weight to doubt on the universal validity of Western (usually American) management theory, since management is very much an American concept, just as earlier the entire discipline of economics was very much an Anglo-Saxon discipline.[60] Consequently, all management theories should be examined for culturally-relative validity in this view. Hofstede widely examines and critiques, in terms of cultural relativism, Western theories relating to motivation, leadership, management by objectives, planning and control, organization design and development, the humanization of work, and industrial democracy and others.[61] Hofstede suggests that Leadership and Industrial Democracy is largely influenced by PDI and IDV in a society. He suggests that 'neither McGregor nor Likert nor Blake and Mouton nor any other U.S. leadership theorists I know has taken the collective values of subordinates into account',[62] and suggests that industrial democracy is basically a contradiction for Chinese organizations, 'in which participative structures in work situations are combined with a strictly controlled hierarchy in ideological issues'.[63]

A similar conclusion is drawn in another article which concludes that high PDI cultures are generally unreceptive to 'participative' management theories.[64] In terms of organization design, Hofstede considers PDI and UAI to be influential in the Aston Studies dimensions of concentration of authority and structuring of activities. Organizations are likely to be 'structured in order to meet the subjective cultural needs of their members.'[65] Hofstede points to a study by Stevens as empirical support for the relationship between PDI-UAI and implicit models of organizations. Hofstede theorizes about an Asian/African addition to this model of culture-based organizational structure, as provided in the work of Stevens, supporting the proposition that this translates into organizational structures of Hong Kong and other Asian firms, which are a distinct form of simple 'personnel bureaucracy'. According to Hofstede,

[the] equivalent implicit model of an organization in these countries is the (extended) 'family', in which the owner-manager is the omnipotent (grand)father. It corresponds to large power distance but weak uncertainty avoidance, a situation in which people would resolve the conflict described by permanent referral to the boss.[66]

In contrast, the implicit structure of organizations in Britain (where PDI and UAI scores are both low), according to Stevens' evidence, was 'a "village market" in which neither hierarchy nor rules, determine what will happen.'[67]

The cultural characteristics of a country affect conceptions of human nature produced in a society, and will influence the managerial theories produced therein. One influence is the degree of individualism which, according to Hofstede, provides an environment where theories of motivation such as those of Maslow are inappropriate for collective societies, in which higher motives are unlikely to be 'self actualization' (as in Anglo-Saxon cultures) but the collective interests and honour of the in-group and harmony, consensus, trust in the society. Real motivators (as opposed to 'hygiene factors' in Hertzberg's terms) are likely to be different in Hong Kong than the UK because of PDI. In Hong Kong, large PDI leading to dependence should be seen as a real motivator as 'the motivator should rather be labelled the "master". He differs from the "boss" in that his power is based on tradition and charisma more than on formal position.'[68] Similar motives might be expected in Hong Kong and the UK, in theory, in terms of McClelland's need for achievement (and esteem), since both countries have a weak UAI and strong MAS scores,[69] although how achievement is interpreted may differ between societies because of differences in long-term orientation, individualism and differences in the nature of masculinity.

Other needs, such as 'respect , harmony, face and duty',[70] are somewhat neglected in the somewhat ethnocentric view of the world, provided by Maslow, McClelland and other Western management theorists, and, as a result, these theories in their original form do not qualify as adequate foundations for a cross-cultural study. This extends to more recent theory also as Hofstede explains the popularity in the US of 'expectancy' theories of motivation, which see people as pulled by the expectancy of outcomes, mostly consciously,[71] as explicable in terms of the assumed 'calculative involvement' of highly individualistic Americans in organizations. By implication, expectancy theories are not considered to be appropriate in a collective society like Hong Kong. Adler[72] adds support to these in suggesting that differences in uncertainty avoidance provide widely different perceptions of motivation, implying that much of the Western theory in this area is culture-bound. Other more recent management theories must be examined to see if they pass the 'test' of cultural relativism implicit in Hofstede's work. In international business and management studies, the justification and potential exists for culturally-based deconstruction of theories originating in the West and claiming universal validity. This is largely a task for subsequent articles, but it should be noted that Hofstede does not consider Peters and Waterman to have fully passed the 'test' of cultural relativity, since their prescriptions for 'excellence' in organizational culture are universal and not environmentally or culturally contingent. Hofstede objects and disagrees with Peters and Waterman's book, *In Search of Excellence*, where eight conditions for excellence are presented as norms. The book suggests there is 'one best way' towards excellence'.[73]

In a similar vein, Redding implies that Porter is seeking to advocate universally applicable theory predicated upon the ethnocentric assumption of competitive market solutions. Redding sees that cultural differences mean different varieties of capitalism and the network market substitutes inherent in OC economies are a manifestation of a very different Chinese way which renders Porters 'models' of little use in East Asia.[74] Having bemoaned the theoretical cross-cultural relevance of a range of management theories, it is important also to recognize that such theories do have an effect in Hong Kong. A cursory glance at *The South China Morning Post* reveals a bewildering array of MBA and other management courses provided by foreign and domestic institutions. If we assume that these popular courses contain mostly a theory of Western origin, then it is clear that such ideas are being studied and used by many Hong Kong managers. It has been suggested that this form of Western management, 'imperial' influence is not simple acculturation as much of the theory borrowed from the West that will be transformed and integrated by passing through the filter of the local culture.[75] For example, theories of marketing relating to market research, the marketing mix and marketing implementation and control are likely to be transformed by the indigenous culture, as are organization theory and behaviour relating to the 'shape' of organizations, the meaning and responses of people at work and the behavioural processes in organizations.[76]

SUMMARY AND CONCLUSIONS

This article reviews the consequences of Hofstede's seminal study of international evaluative cultural differences for management in Hong Kong. Support for Hofstede's proposition that management is inherently culture-bound is reviewed after the approach to culture adopted by Hofstede is evaluated. Hofstede's idea that implicit models of organization and modal organizational structure are culturally contingent is explored in some depth and supportive models from eclectic sources are reviewed, in order to provide theoretical support for this aspect of the 'culture-bound' hypothesis. Hong Kong culture is also reviewed both in terms of its position regarding both 'etic' dimensions and 'emic' idiosyncracies. In conclusion, in answering the principal question posed by Hofstede: 'Do American theories apply abroad?' in the context of Hong Kong, we can answer in a qualified way. It seems that many American and Western theories are culture-bound and of dubious value without modification for local cultural characteristics. Yet Western management courses have never been so popular in Hong Kong as evidenced by the ubiquitous MBA . The Western theories inherent in these courses will, however, have to pass through local cultural 'filters' and are unlikely to be received or used by Chinese managers in the way that their Western architects intended, as they are likely to be indigenized to solve the idiosyncratic problems of managers in Hong Kong. Perhaps the appropriate question should now be 'How should American management theories be applied in Hong Kong?'

NOTES

1. M. Sondergaard, 'Research Note: Hofstede's Consequences: A Study of Reviews, Citations and Replications', *Organisation Studies*, Vol.15/3 (1994), pp.447–56.
2. G. Hofstede, *Culture's Consequences* (1980).
3. M. Sondergaard, 'Research Note', p.451.
4. S. Lowe, 'Hermes Revisited: A Replication of Hofstede's Study in Hong Kong and The UK', *Asia Pacific Business Review*, Vol.2, No.3 (Spring, 1996), pp.101–19.
5. Hofstede, 'Culture's Consequences', p.15.
6. Ibid., p.32.
7. Ibid., p.34.
8. C. Kerr *et. al., Industrialism and Industrial Man* (1960).
9. Sondergaard, 'Research Note'.
10. Hofstede, 'Culture's Consequences', p.22.
11. J.W. Berry *et. al., Cross-Cultural Psychology: Research and Applications* (1992), p.12.
12. Hofstede, 'Culture's Consequences', p.23.
13. H.S.R. Kao *et. al., Effective Organisations and Social Values* (1994), p.18.
14. S.G. Redding , *The Spirit of Chinese Capitalism* (1990), p.12.
15. D. Sinha and H.S.R. Kao (eds), *Social Values and Development : Asian Perspectives* (1990).
16. P. Di Maggio, 'Nadel's Paradox Revisited: Relational and Cultural Aspects of Organisational Structure' in Nohria and Eccles (eds), *Networks and Organisations ; Structure, Form, and Action* (1992).
17. Ibid., p.110.
18. A. Giddens, *The Constitution of Society* (1984).
19. Di Maggio, 'Nadel's Paradox Revisited'.
20. F. Trompenaars, *Riding the Waves of Culture* (1993).
21. Hampden-Turner and Trompenaars, *The Seven Cultures of Capitalism* (1994).
22. Kao *et al.*, 'Effective Organisations', p.12.
23. M. Chen, *Asian Management Systems: Chinese, Japanese and Korean Styles of Management* (1995).
24. P.Y. Huo and D.M. Randall, 'Exploring Subcultural Differences in Hofstede's Value Survey: The Case of The Chinese', *Asia Pacific Journal of Management,*Vol.8, No.2 (1991), pp.159–73.
25. Lowe, 'Hermes Revisited'.
26. G.Y.Y. Wong and Birnbaum-More, 'Culture, Context and Structure: A Test on Hong Kong Banks', *Organisation Studies*, Vol 15, No.1 (1994), pp.99–123.
27. H. Colebatch and P. Larmour, *Market, Bureaucracy and Community: A Student's Guide to Organisation* (1993).
28. S.C. Schneider, 'Strategy Formulation: The Impact of National Culture', *Organisation Studies*, Vol.10, No.2 (1989), pp.149–68.
29. A. Laurent, 'The Cultural Diversity of Western Concepts of Management', *International Studies of Management and Organisation*, Vol.12, Nos.1–2 (1983), pp.75–96.
30. M. Taylor, *Community, Anarchy and Liberty* (1982).
31. H. Colebatch and P.Larmour, 'Market, Bureaucracy and Community', p.22.
32. G. Thompson *et al.* (eds.), *Markets, Hierarchies and Networks : The Coordination of Social Life* (1991); R.Marchment and G.Thompson (eds), *Managing the UK: An Introduction to its Political Economy and Public Policy* (1993); J.C. Jarillo, 'On Strategic Networks', *Strategic Management Journal*, Vol.9 (1988), pp.31–41; C.Handy, *Gods of Management* (1985) .
33. O.E. Williamson, *Markets and Hierarchies* (1975).
34. W. Ouchi, 'Markets, Bureaucracies and Clans', *Administrative Science Quarterly*, Vol.25(1)

(1980), pp.129–41.
35. F. Tonnies, *Gemeinschaft and Gesellschaft (Community and Society)* (1957), trans. C. Loomis.
36. G. Wong, 'Business Groups in a Dynamic Environment: Hong Kong 1976–1986' in G. Hamilton (ed.), *Business Networks and Economic Development in East and South East Asia* (University of Hong Kong papers, 1991).
37. M. Boisot, *Information and Organisations: The Manager as Anthropologist* (1987).
38. M. Douglas, *Natural Symbols : Explorations in Cosmology* (1973).
39. G. Hofstede, *Culture and Organisations* (1991), p.149.
40. M. Douglas *et al.*, 'Institutions of the Third Kind' in *Risk and Blame* (1992).
41. J. Scott, 'Corporate Interlocks and Social Network Analysis', SSRC Occasional paper 8 (University of Hong Kong, 1992), p.20.
42. Redding, 'Spirit of Chinese Capitalism', p.12.
43. Ibid., p.15.
44. Ibid.
45. G. Hamilton and N.W. Biggart, 'Market, Culture and Authority: A Comparative Analysis of Management and Organisation in the Far East', *American Journal of Sociology*, Vol.94 (1988), pp.552–94; G.Hamilton and C.S. Kao, 'The Institutional Foundation of Chinese Business: the Family Firm in Taiwan', *Comparative Social Research*, Vol.12 (1990), pp.95–112; R. Whitley, *Business Systems in East Asia: Firms, Markets and Societies* (1992).
46. Williamson, 'Markets and Hierarchies'.
47. S.C. Schneider, 'Strategy Formulation: The Impact of National Culture', *Organisation Studies*, Vol.10/2 (1989), p.153.
48. R.I. Westwood, *Organisation Behaviour: Southeast Asian Perspectives* (1992).
49. Ibid., pp.112–15.
50. Ibid., p.51.
51. H. Bedi , *Understanding The Asian Manager* (1991), p.2.
52. J.-C. Spender, *Industry Recipes : The Nature and Sources of Management Judgement* (1989).
53. This term refers to a somewhat contentious model of traditional societies proposed by J.C. Scott, *The Moral Economy of the Peasant* (1976).
54. The role of 'guanxi' or relationships as a control alternative to the rule of law in Taiwan is articulated in Jane Kaufman Winn in *The Other Taiwan: 1945 to the Present* (1995), edited by M. A. Rubenstein.
55. Redding, 'Spirit of Chinese Capitalism'.
56. E. Chen and G. Hamilton, 'Introduction: Business Networks and Economic Development' in Hamilton (ed.), 'Business Networks'.
57. S.-L. Wong, 'Chinese Entrepreneurs and Business Trust' in Hamilton, 'Business Networks'; T.R. Pyatt and C.C.-H. Kwok, 'The Nature of South East Asian Business Networks and Buyer Behaviour', and D.Yeung and C.K.C.Kenneth, 'Marketing and Purchasing Strategies in the Life Insurance Industry of Hong Kong' in 'Asian Success and International Business Theory', Proceedings of AIB Western and Southeast Asian Regional Meeting, June 1993.
58. S.G. Redding, 'Cultural Effects on the Marketing Process in Southeast Asia', *Journal of the Market Research Society*, Vol.24, No.2 (1982), pp.98–122.
59. C. Gronroos, *Service Management and Marketing: Managing the Moment of Truth in Service Competition* (1989).
60. Hofstede, 'Culture's Consequences', p.253.
61. Ibid., ch. 9.
62. Ibid., p.259.
63. Ibid., p.269.
64. N. Adler, *International Dimensions of Organisational Behaviour* (1991).
65. G.Hofstede, *Culture and Organisations* (1991), p.142.
66. Ibid., p.143.
67. Ibid., p.142.
68. Ibid., p154.
69. Ibid., p.124.
70. Ibid., p.126.
71. Hofstede, 'Culture's Consequences', p.255.
72. Adler, 'International Dimensions'.
73. Hofstede, 'Culture and Organisations', p.199.
74. S.G. Redding, 'Competitive Advantage in the Context of Hong Kong', *Journal of Far Eastern Business*, Vol.1. No.1 (Autumn 1994).
75. J.-C. Usunier, *International Marketing : A Cultural Approach* (1993), p 11.
76. Westwood, 'Organisation Behaviour'.